MENTAL HEALTH AND SUBSTANCE ABUSE RECOVERY

AUTHOR JAMES E. DEAN

Copyright © 2020 by James E. Dean. All Rights Reserved.

No part of this publication may be reproduced, distributed, or transmitted in any form or by any means, including photocopying, recording, or other electronic or mechanical methods, or by any information storage and retrieval system without the prior written permission of Smith Show Publishing, except in the case of very brief quotations embodied in critical reviews and certain other noncommercial uses permitted by copyright law.

TABLE OF CONTENTS

RECOVERY STRATEGIES……………………..……..3
FACTS ABOUT SCHIZOPHRENIA…….………..29
FACTS ABOUT BIPOLAR DISORDER…..…….60
FACTS ABOUT DEPRESSION…………………….89
STRESS MODELS AND TREATMENTS…..112
BUILDING SOCIAL SUPPORT……..……….….159
DRUG AND ALCOHOL USE……………….…...201
REDUCING REPAPSES………………...............232
COPING WITH STRESS………………..............260
COPING WITH PROBLEMS AND SYMPTOMS…………………………….................292
GETTING YOUR NEEDS MET IN THE MENTAL HEALTH SYSTEM…………….…332
NOTES…………………………………………………....355

Recovery Strategies

CHAPTER 1

Introduction

This workbook is about the topic of recovery from mental illness. It includes a discussion of how different people define recovery and encourages each person to develop his or her own definition of recovery. Pursuing goals is an important part of the recovery process. Working on this handout can help you set recovery goals and choose strategies to pursue these goals.

What is "recovery"?

People define recovery from mental illness in their own individual ways. Some people think of it as a process, while others think of it as a goal or an end result.

Here are some examples of how different people describe recovery from their own point of view:

- "Recovery from mental illness is not like recovery from the flu. It's recovering your life and your identity."
- "Recovery for me is having good relationships and feeling connected. It's being able to enjoy my life."
- "I don't dwell on the past. I'm focusing on my future."
- "Being more independent is an important part of my recovery process."
- "Not having symptoms any more is my definition of recovery."

- "Recovery for me is a series of steps. Sometimes the steps are small, like fixing lunch, taking a walk, following my daily routine. Small steps add up."
- "Having a mental illness is part of my life, but not the center of my life."
- "Recovery is about having confidence and self-esteem. I have something positive to offer the world."

> *People define recovery in their own personal ways.*

<u>Question</u>: What does recovery mean to you?

What helps people in the process of recovery?

People use a variety of different strategies to help themselves in the recovery process, such as the following:

Becoming involved in self-help programs

"I belong to a support group which is part of a self-help program. Everyone in the group has experienced psychiatric symptoms. I feel very comfortable there. The other people understand what I am going through. They also have good ideas for solving certain problems."

(Contact information for a variety of self help programs and resources is provided in the Appendix to this handout).

Staying active

"I find that the more I do to stay active during the day, the better things go. I make a list each day of what I want to do. I try to list fun things as well as work things. Just being active makes me feel more confident."

Developing a support system

"It helps me to have friends and family I can do things with and talk things over with. Sometimes I have to work on these relationships and make sure I stay in touch. It's better for me not to rely on just one person."

Maintaining physical health

"When I've been eating junk food or not getting any exercise, it makes me feel sluggish, both physically and mentally. So I try to eat things that have decent nutrition and I try to get at least a little exercise every day. It makes a lot of difference."

Being aware of the environment and how it affects you

"I concentrate much better when I'm in a quiet environment. When things start to get noisy I get distracted and sometimes I get irritable. When I can, I seek out quieter places and situations with fewer people involved. It also upsets me to be around critical people. I avoid that kind of person when I can."

Making time for leisure and recreation

"I can't just work all the time. I need time for pleasure, too. My wife and I like to rent a video every Friday. We take turns picking out what we will watch."

Creativity

"I like to write poetry. It helps me to express my emotions and put my experiences into words. And sometimes I read other people's poems. It's very satisfying."

Spirituality

"Being in touch with my spirituality is essential to me. I belong to a church, but I also find spirituality in meditation and in nature."

Following through with treatment choices

"I have chosen treatment that includes a self-help group, a part-time job, and taking medication. I like to be pro-active. Following through with those things makes me feel strong, like I can handle my daily challenges."

"I'm in a peer support program, and I see a therapist once a week who helps me figure out how to deal with some of the problems in my life. Both things have been important to my recovery."

Strategies for recovery include:

- *self-help programs*
- *staying active*
- *developing a support system*
- *maintaining physical health*
- *being aware of the environment*
- *making time for recreation*
- *expressing creativity*
- *seeking out spirituality*
- *following through with treatment choices.*

Questions: Which of the strategies for recovery have you used?
Which of the strategies would you like to develop further or try out?
You can use the following chart to record your answers to these questions.

Strategies for Recovery

Strategy	I already use this strategy	I would like to try this strategy or develop it further
Self help programs		
Staying active		
Developing a support system		
Maintaining physical health		
Being aware of the environment		
Making time for recreation		
Expressing creativity		
Expressing spirituality		
Following through with my treatment choices (such as: _____)		
Other:		

What's important to you? What goals would you like to pursue?

Most people in the process of recovery report that it is important to establish and pursue goals, whether the goals are small or large. However, experiencing psychiatric symptoms can take up a great deal of your time and energy. Sometimes this can make it difficult to participate in activities or even to figure out what you would like to do.

It may be helpful to take some time to review what's important to you as an individual, what you want to accomplish and what you want your life to be like. The following questions may be helpful:

- What kind of friendships would you like to have?
- What would you like to do with your spare time?
- What kind of hobbies or sports or activities would you like to participate in?
- What kind of work (paid or volunteer) would you like to be doing?
- Are there any classes you would like to take?
- What kind of close relationship would you like to have?
- What kind of living situation would you like to have?
- Would you like to change your financial situation?
- How would you like to express your creativity?
- What kind of relationships would you like with your family?
- What kind of spiritual community would you like to belong to?

It may also be helpful to think about the following questions:

- Which areas of life do I feel most satisfied with?
- Which areas of life do I feel least satisfied with?
- What would I like to change?

The following chart may help you answer these questions:

Satisfaction with Areas of My life

Area of my life	I am not satisfied	I am moderately satisfied	I am very satisfied
Friendships			
Meaningful work (paid or unpaid)			
Enjoyable activities			
Family relationships			
Living situation			
Spirituality			
Finances			
Belonging to a community			
Intimate relationships			
Expressing creativity			
Hobbies or activities for fun			
Education			
Other area:			

You might find it helpful to set goals for yourself in one or two areas of your life that you are not satisfied with. For example, if you are not satisfied with having enough enjoyable activities, it might be a good idea to set a goal of identifying some activities and scheduling time to try them out.

> *Identifying what you would like to improve in your life will help you set goals.*

Question: What two areas of your life are you not satisfied with and would like to improve?
What goals would you like to set for yourself in these areas? You can use the following chart to record your goals. You can also refer back to the chart to record how you follow up on these goals.

Goals Set in the Illness Management and Recovery Program

Date goal was Set	Goal	Follow-up

What are some strategies for achieving your goals?

Setting goals

People who are most effective at getting what they want usually set clear goals for themselves and plan step-by-step what they are going to do.

The following suggestions may be helpful:

- Break down large goals into smaller, more manageable ones.

- Start with short-term goals that are relatively modest and that are likely to be achieved.

- Focus on one goal at a time.

- Get support in working on goals; other people's ideas and participation can make a big difference.

- Don't be discouraged if it takes longer than you think to accomplish a goal; this is very common.

- If you first attempt to achieve a goal doesn't work, don't lose heart and give up. Keep trying other strategies until you find something that works. As the saying goes, "If at first you don't succeed, try, try again!"

Planning steps for achieving goals

You may find it helpful to follow a step-by-step method, such as the following, for achieving goals. This method can also be used to solve problems, as described in the handout "Coping with Problems and Symptoms."

1. Define the goal you would like to accomplish. Be as specific as possible.

2. List at least 3 possible ways to achieve the goal.

3. For each possibility, briefly evaluate its advantages (the pros) and disadvantages (the cons) for achieving your goal.

4. Choose the best way to achieve your goal. Be as practical as possible.

5. Plan the steps for carrying out your decision. Think about: Who will be involved? What step will each person do? What is the time frame? What resources are needed? What problems might come up and how could they be overcome?

6. Set a date for evaluating how well your plan is working. First focus on the positive: What has been accomplished? What went well? Then look at whether your goal has been achieved. If it hasn't been achieved, decide whether to revise your plan or try another one.

> *Make a step-by-step plan to help you achieve your goals.*

Questions: What is an example of a goal that you have set in the past?
Have you used a step-by-step plan for achieving a goal before?

What goals would you like to focus on?

Choose one or two goals that you would like to achieve. Start with goals that are relatively small and have a strong chance of being successful. Use the following planning sheets to record your plans.

Working on Goals

Goal #_____

[ ]

First Steps toward the Goal*

[ ]

Goal #_____

[ ]

First Steps toward the Goal*

[ ]

*Significant obstacles might best be solved by first using the *Problem-Solving Model* found in the appendix of **Educational Handout #1.**

Step-by-Step Problem-Solving and Goal Achievement

1. Define the problem or goal as specifically and simply as possible.

2. List 3 possible ways to solve the problem or achieve the goal:
   a.
   b.
   c.

3. For each possibility, list one advantage and one disadvantage:
 	
Advantages/pros: Disadvantages/cons:
   a.   a.
   b.   b.
   c.   c.

4. Choose the best way to solve the problem or achieve the goal. Which way has the best chance of succeeding?

5. Plan the steps for carrying out the solution. Who will be involved? What step will each person do? What is the time frame? What resources are needed? What problems might come up? How could they be overcome?
   a.
   b.
   c.
   d.
   e.
   f.

6. Set a date for follow up:_____. Give yourself credit for what you have done. Decide whether the problem has been solved or whether the goal has been achieved. If not, decide whether to revise the plan or try another one.

Step-by-Step Problem-Solving and Goal Achievement

1. Define the problem or goal as specifically and simply as possible.

2. List 3 possible ways to solve the problem or achieve the goal:
   a.
   b.
   c.

3. For each possibility, list one advantage and one disadvantage:
 	
   Advantages/pros: Disadvantages/cons:
   a.   a.
   b.   b.
   c.   c.

4. Choose the best way to solve the problem or achieve the goal. Which way has the best chance of succeeding?

5. Plan the steps for carrying out the solution. Who will be involved? What step will each person do? What is the time frame? What resources are needed? What problems might come up? How could they be overcome?
   a.
   b.
   c.
   d.
   e.
   f.

6. Set a date for follow up:_____. Give yourself credit for what you have done. Decide whether the problem has been solved or whether the goal has been achieved. If not, decide whether to revise the plan or try another one.

What reminders, guidelines or suggestions to yourself will help you most in pursuing your recovery goals?

James's recovery goals center on working and being a good husband and father. He uses the following reminders for himself:

- Make time for yourself.
- Reward yourself for things you do.
- Look good for yourself.
- Keep up with your appointments.
- Tell people what's really on your mind.
- Try to listen to your doctor and nurse.
- Think positively. Have hope.
- Get outside those four walls—take a walk, see a movie, go listen to music in the park.
- Make time for romance.
- Learn what makes you feel good, what you enjoy doing.
- Be willing to apologize sometimes; it takes a real man or a real woman to apologize.
- You don't have to get in arguments with people who say things you don't like. It only builds up your adrenaline, and then you feel worse.
- Say a prayer. "Let me be positive today. Don't let me focus on the negative."

In David's recovery, he has focused on goals related to creative expression, living independently and having strong relationships with family and friends. He said that the following guidelines have helped him pursue his goals:

- Express yourself in art. Do it for your own enjoyment.
- Express yourself in writing. Keep a journal. Write a poem, a story, an article, or even a comic.
- Find a job that suits you and is not too stressful.
- Stay busy. Try to schedule things with other people.
- Persist until you find a medication that's right for you.
- Don't let other people's opinions about mental illness get you down.
- Meet other people who have experienced psychiatric symptoms.
- Help other people in their recovery. You'll both feel the benefits.
- Keep up family traditions as much as possible and stay in touch with family members.

Sarah said that her recovery goals center on improving her relationships with the important people in her life (her husband, best friend, and mother) and maintaining her good social standing in the community. She said that finding out who she is and what she likes has been her salvation. For Sarah, a daily checklist has been important in pursuing her recovery goals. She suggests asking yourself the following questions every morning:

- How is your medication situation?
- How is your wardrobe?
- Did you eat a healthy breakfast?
- What is your structure for the day?
- How is your money situation?
- Who do you trust, who can you talk to?
- Are you getting good sleep?

Each person finds his or her own pathway to recovery.

What reminders, guidelines, or suggestions to yourself will help you most in pursuing your recovery goals?
1.
2.
3.
4.
5.

Summary of the main points about recovery strategies:

People define recovery in their own personal ways.

- *Strategies for recovery include:*
    - *Self help programs*
    - *Staying active*
    - *Developing a support system*
    - *Maintaining physical health*
    - *Being aware of the environment and how it affects you*
    - *Making time for leisure and recreation*
    - *Expressing creativity*
    - *Seeking out spirituality*
    - *Following through with treatment choices*

- *Identifying what you would like to improve in your life will help you set goals.*

- *Make a step-by-step plan to help you achieve your goals.*

- *Each person finds his or her own pathway to recovery.*

Mental Illness Education Project (MIEP)
800-343-5540.
website: miepvideos.org.
The Mental Illness Education Project seeks to improve understanding of mental illness through the production of video-based programs for use by people with psychiatric conditions, their families, mental health practitioners, administrators, and educators, as well as the general public.

Mental Health Recovery
802-254-2092
website: mentalhealthrecovery.com
Mary Ellen Copeland has developed a number of publications and programs for helping people in the recovery process, including the Wellness Recovery Action Plan (WRAP). Her web site offers a free newsletter and articles and a list of publications and workshops that can be purchased.

National Alliance for the Mentally Ill (NAMI)
800-950-NAMI (helpline). www.nami.org.
NAMI is a support and advocacy organization of consumers, families and friends of people with mental illness. It provides educational about severe brain disorders, supports increased funding for research and advocates for adequate health

Working on Goals

Goal #_____

```
[                                                    ]
```

First Steps toward the Goal*

```
[                                                    ]
```

Goal #_____

```
[                                                    ]
```

First Steps toward the Goal*

```
[                                                    ]
```

*Significant obstacles might best be solved by first using the *Problem-Solving Model* found in the appendix of **Educational Handout #1.**

Step-by-Step Problem-Solving and Goal Achievement

1. Define the problem or goal as specifically and simply as possible.

2. List 3 possible ways to solve the problem or achieve the goal:
  a.
  b.
  c.

3. For each possibility, list one advantage and one disadvantage:
 	
Advantages/pros: Disadvantages/cons:
  a.   a.
  b.   b.
  c.   c.

4. Choose the best way to solve the problem or achieve the goal. Which way has the best chance of succeeding?

5. Plan the steps for carrying out the solution. Who will be involved? What step will each person do? What is the time frame? What resources are needed? What problems might come up? How could they be overcome?
  a.
  b.
  c.
  d.
  e.
  f.

6. Set a date for follow up:_____. Give yourself credit for what you have done. Decide whether the problem has been solved or whether the goal has been achieved. If not, decide whether to revise the plan or try another one.

Facts about Schizophrenia

CHAPTER 2

Introduction

This handout provides information about the psychiatric disorder of schizophrenia. Facts are given about how a diagnosis is made, the symptoms, how common it is, and the possible courses of the disorder. Several examples are included of famous people who have experienced the symptoms of schizophrenia and have made positive contributions to society.

What is schizophrenia?

Schizophrenia is a major mental disorder that affects many people. About one in every one hundred people (1%) develops the disorder at some time in his or her life. It occurs in every country, every culture, every racial group and at every income level.

Schizophrenia causes symptoms that can interfere with many aspects of people's lives, especially their work and social life. Some symptoms make it difficult to know what's real and what's not real. These symptoms have been described as being similar to "dreaming when you are wide awake." Other symptoms can cause problems with motivation, concentration, and experiencing enjoyment.

It is important to know that there are many reasons to be optimistic about the future:

- There is effective treatment for schizophrenia.
- People with schizophrenia can learn to manage their illness.
- People with schizophrenia can lead productive lives.

The more you understand about the illness and take an active role in your treatment, the better you will feel and the more you can accomplish toward your life goals.

Schizophrenia is a major psychiatric disorder that affects many aspects of a person's life.

---

1 in every 100 people develops schizophrenia at some point in his or her life.

People can learn to manage the symptoms of schizophrenia and lead productive lives.

Question: What did you know about schizophrenia before you had personal experience with it?

How is schizophrenia diagnosed?

Schizophrenia is diagnosed based on a clinical interview conducted by a specially trained professional, usually a doctor, but sometimes a nurse, psychologist, social worker or other mental health practitioner. In the interview, there are questions about symptoms you have experienced and how you are functioning in different areas of your life, such as relationships and work.

There is currently no blood test, X-ray, or brain scan that can be used to diagnose schizophrenia. To make an accurate diagnosis, however, the doctor may also request a physical exam and certain lab tests or blood tests in order to rule out other causes of symptoms, such as a brain tumor or an injury to the brain.

Schizophrenia is diagnosed by a clinical interview with a mental health professional.

Question: How long did it take for a mental health professional to accurately diagnose the symptoms you experienced?

What are the symptoms of schizophrenia?

It is important to keep in mind that the symptoms of schizophrenia can be found in other mental disorders. Specifying a diagnosis of schizophrenia is based on a combination of different symptoms, how long they have been present, and their severity. Symptoms that occur only when a person has used alcohol or drugs are not included.

No one has the exact same symptoms or is bothered to the same degree. You may, however, recognize having experienced some of the following symptoms:

"Hallucinations" are false perceptions. This means that people hear, see, feel or smell something that is not actually there. Hearing voices is the most common type of hallucination.

Some voices might be pleasant, but many times they are unpleasant, saying insulting things or calling people names. When people hear voices, it seems like the sound is coming in through their ears and the voices sound like other human voices. It sounds extremely real.

Some examples:

- "A voice kept criticizing me and telling me that I was a bad person."
- "Sometimes I heard two voices talking about me and commenting on what I was doing."

Many people also experience visual hallucinations, which involves seeing things that are not there.

Some examples:

- "Once I saw a lion standing in the doorway to my bedroom. It looked so real."
- "I thought I saw fire coming in the window. No one else saw it."

"Delusions" are false beliefs. This means that people have strong beliefs that are firmly held and unshakeable, even when there is evidence that contradicts them. These beliefs are very individual, and not shared by others in their culture or religion. Delusions seem very real to the person experiencing them, but they seem impossible and untrue to others.

One common delusion is when people believe that others want to hurt them, when they don't (paranoid delusion). Another common delusion is people believing that they have special powers, talents or wealth. Other delusions include people believing that another person or force can control their thoughts or actions, or believing that others are referring to them or talking about them.

Some examples:

- "I believed that someone was trying to poison me."
- "I was convinced that the TV was talking about me."
- "I believed that I was fantastically wealthy, in spite of the balance in my bank account."
- "I thought that people were reading my thoughts."
- "No matter what the doctor said, I was convinced that I had parasites."

A "thought disorder" is confused thinking. This symptom makes it difficult to stay on the topic, use the correct words, form complete sentences, or talk in an organized way that other people can understand.

Some examples:

- "People told me I jumped from topic to topic. They said I wasn't making sense."
- "I used to make up words when describing things to my brother, but he said he didn't understand what I was saying."
- "I'd be talking and suddenly I would stop in the middle of a thought and couldn't continue. It was like I something was blocking my thought."

"Cognitive difficulties" are problems with concentration, memory and abstract reasoning. This means that people might have problems with paying attention, remembering things, and understanding concepts.

Some examples:

- "I had trouble concentrating on reading or watching TV."
- "I couldn't remember plans or appointments."
- "I had problems understanding abstract ideas."

A "decline in social or occupational functioning" means spending much less time socializing with other people or being unable to work or go to school. This symptom is especially important, because it must be present for at least 6 months in order to diagnose schizophrenia. It is also important because it has a big impact on people being able to carry out their roles in a wide variety of areas, such as taking care of themselves or their children or their household responsibilities.

Some examples:

- "It became very uncomfortable to spend time with people. I went from loving to go out with friends to dreading it and avoiding it whenever I could."
- "I couldn't do the cooking and cleaning any more. Everyday household tasks became absolutely overwhelming to me."
- "My job was very important to me, but it became increasingly impossible to do it. I tried very hard, but I had trouble with even the most basic tasks. It was very hard to explain to anyone."

"Disorganized or catatonic behavior" refers to two different extremes of behavior. Both are relatively rare. "Disorganized behavior" is behavior that appears random or purposeless to others. "Catatonic behavior" refers to when a person stops almost all movement and is immobile (or almost completely immobile) for long periods of time.

An example of disorganized behavior:

- "I used to spend whole days moving all the pots and pans from the kitchen to the basement to the bathroom then back to the kitchen. Then I'd start all over again."

An example of catatonic behavior:

- "I don't remember this, but my brother told me that before I started getting help, I used to sit in the same chair for hours and hours. I wouldn't move a muscle, not even to take a drink of water."

"Negative symptoms" are the lack of energy, motivation, pleasure and expressiveness.
Negative symptoms lead to people having problems with initiating and following through with plans, being interested in and enjoying things they used to like, and expressing their emotions to others with their facial expression and voice tone. While these symptoms may be accompanied by feelings of sadness, often they are not.

While others may call these symptoms a sign of laziness, it is NOT laziness.

Some examples:

- "I stopped caring about how I looked. I even stopped taking a shower."
- "It was so hard to start a conversation with people, even when I liked them."
- "I didn't have the energy to go to work or go out with friends or follow through with plans."
- "Things that used to be fun, like bowling, didn't seem fun anymore."
- "People told me they couldn't tell what I was feeling. They said they couldn't read my expression. Even when I was interested in what they were saying, they thought I was bored or uninterested."

The major symptoms of schizophrenia are:

- *hallucinations*
- *delusions*
- *thought disorders*
- *cognitive difficulties*
- *decline in social or occupational functioning*
- *disorganized or catatonic behavior*
- *negative symptoms (lack of energy, motivation, pleasure or emotional expression)*

No one has exactly the same symptoms or experiences them to the same degree.

<u>Question</u>: Which of the symptoms have you experienced? You can use the following checklist to record your answer.

Experiences of symptoms of schizophrenia

Symptom	I had this symptom	Example of what happened to me
Hallucinations (hearing, seeing, feeling or smelling something that is not there)		
Delusions (having a strong belief that is firmly held in spite of contrary evidence)		
Thought disorder (difficulty with thinking clearly and expressing myself clearly)		
Cognitive difficulties (problems with concentration, memory and reasoning)		
Decline in social or occupation functioning (less time socializing, problems doing work)		

Disorganized or catatonic behavior (random behavior or remaining motionless)		
Negative symptoms (lack of energy, motivation, pleasure, and emotional expressiveness)		

What causes schizophrenia?

Schizophrenia is nobody's fault. This means that you did not cause the disorder, and neither did your family members or anyone else. Scientists believe that the symptoms of schizophrenia are caused by a chemical imbalance in the brain. Chemicals called "neurotransmitters" send messages in the brain. When they are out of balance, they can cause the brain to send messages that contain wrong information.

Scientists do not know what causes this chemical imbalance, but they believe that whatever causes it happens before birth. This means that some people have a "biological vulnerability" to develop schizophrenia, which then develops at a later age.

In addition to biological vulnerability, stress is also believed to play a role in the onset of schizophrenia and the course of the disorder. The theory of how vulnerability and stress interact with each other is called the "stress-vulnerability model" and is covered in more detail in the handout "The Stress-Vulnerability Model and Treatment Strategies."

Many questions about schizophrenia remain unanswered. There are many research projects underway to try to learn more about the disorder.

> *Schizophrenia is nobody's fault.*

> *Scientists believe that schizophrenia is caused by a chemical imbalance in the brain.*

Question: What other explanations have you heard about what causes schizophrenia?

What is the course of schizophrenia? What happens after you first develop symptoms?

Most people develop schizophrenia as teenagers or young adults, approximately age 16 to age 30. People vary in how often they have symptoms, the severity of their symptoms and how much the disorder interferes with their lives.

Schizophrenia affects people in very different ways. Some people have a milder form of the disorder and only have symptoms a few times in their lives. Other people have a stronger form and have several episodes, some of which require hospitalization. Some people experience symptoms almost constantly, but do not have severe episodes that require hospitalization.

Schizophrenia tends to be episodic, with symptoms varying in intensity over time. When symptoms reappear or get worse, this is usually referred to as a "symptom exacerbation" or an "acute episode" or a "relapse." (More information on this subject is provided in the handout "Reducing Relapses.") Some relapses can be managed at home, but other relapses may require hospitalization to protect the person or others.

With effective treatment most people with schizophrenia can reduce their symptoms and live productive, meaningful lives.

> *Schizophrenia tends to be episodic, with symptoms coming and going at varying levels of intensity.*

Question: What has been your experience with symptom relapses?

Examples of people who have schizophrenia

Some famous people have developed schizophrenia:

John Nash (1928 to present) is an American mathematician who made discoveries in math that had very important applications in the field of Economics. He won the Nobel Prize for Economics in 1994. His story is told in <u>A Beautiful Mind</u>, a book that has also been made into a movie.

William Chester Minor (1834 to 1920) was an American Army surgeon who also had vast knowledge of the English language and literature. He made major contributions to the Oxford English Dictionary, the most comprehensive dictionary in the world.

Vaslav Nijinski (1890 to 1950) was a Russian dancer who is legendary because of his physical strength, light movements and expressive body language. He is especially remembered for a dance piece called "Afternoon of a Faun."

Other people who have developed schizophrenia are not famous, but are quietly leading productive, creative, meaningful lives:

Mr. X: works in an art supply store. He has a close relationship with his two brothers and goes bowling with them regularly. He likes to draw and plans to take an evening art class in the coming year.

Ms. Y: is married and has two children in elementary school. She participates in the home and school association and enjoys gardening.

Mr. Z: lives in a group home and volunteers at the zoo. He used to need frequent hospitalizations, but has successfully stayed out of the hospital for 2 years. He is looking for paid employment.

> *There are countless positive examples of people with schizophrenia who have contributed to society.*

<u>Questions</u>: Do you know other people with schizophrenia?
If so, what are some examples of their personal strengths?

What is stigma?

When referring to mental illness, the word "stigma" means the negative opinions and attitudes that some people have about mental illness. Not everyone with mental illness has experienced stigma, although unfortunately, many have.

It is important to know that there are two major laws that protect against discrimination against people with physical or psychiatric disabilities. The Americans with Disabilities Act (ADA) makes it illegal to discriminate in the areas of employment, transportation, communication or recreation. The Fair Housing Act (FHA) prohibits housing discrimination.

Stigma is a complicated problem, and there are no easy solutions. Research has shown that as the general public gets to know more about mental disorders and as they get to know people who have experienced psychiatric symptoms, their negative beliefs go down.

Many organizations, including the National Institute of Mental Health, the Center for Mental Health Services, the National Alliance for the Mentally Ill, the National Mental Health Association, and the National Empowerment Center, are working on national campaigns to educate the public and create more laws that protect against discrimination. Contact information for these organizations is listed in the Appendix of the "Recovery Strategies" handout.

If you have experienced stigma and/or would like to know more about strategies for responding to stigma, refer to the Appendix to this handout.

> *Stigma refers to negative opinions and attitudes about mental illness.*

Question: Have you ever experienced stigma because of psychiatric symptoms?

What are some of the steps you can take to manage your symptoms?

By reading this handout, you are already taking an important step, which is to learn some practical facts about your disorder.

Other important steps include:

- Learning how to cope with stress
- Building social support
- Developing a relapse prevention plan
- Using medication effectively
- Learning how to cope with symptoms
- Getting your needs met in the mental health system

These steps will be covered in the other educational handouts in the Illness Management and Recovery Program.

> *What you do makes a difference in your recovery.*

> *There are steps you can take to manage psychiatric symptoms effectively.*

Summary of the main points about schizophrenia:

- *Schizophrenia is a major psychiatric disorder that affects many aspects of a person's life.*

- *1 in every 100 people develops schizophrenia at some point in his or her life.*

- *People can learn to manage the symptoms of schizophrenia and lead productive lives.*

- *Schizophrenia is diagnosed by a clinical interview with a mental health professional.*

- *The major symptoms of schizophrenia are:*

    Hallucinations
    > Delusions
    > Thought disorders
    > Cognitive difficulties
    > Decline in social or occupational functioning
    > Disorganized or catatonic behavior
    > Negative symptoms (lack of energy, motivation, pleasure or emotional expression)

- *No one has exactly the same symptoms or experiences them to the same degree.*

- *Schizophrenia is nobody's fault.*

- *Scientists believe that schizophrenia is caused by a chemical imbalance in the brain.*

- *Schizophrenia tends to be episodic, with symptoms coming and going at varying levels of intensity.*

- *There are countless positive examples of people with schizophrenia who have contributed to society.*

- *Stigma refers to negative opinions and attitudes about mental illness.*

- *What you do makes a difference in your recovery.*

- *There are steps you can take to manage psychiatric symptoms effectively.*

Appendix: Strategies and Resources for Responding to Stigma

What are some strategies for responding to stigma?

It may be helpful for you to develop some personal strategies for responding to stigma. There are advantages and disadvantages to each strategy. What you decide to do depends on the specific situation.

Some possible strategies include:

Educate yourself about mental disorders

Sometimes people who experience psychiatric symptoms do not know the facts themselves. They may blame themselves for their symptoms or think they cannot take care of themselves or that they can't be part of the community. You may have had these negative thoughts or feelings. This is called "self-stigma."

It is important to fight self-stigma, because it can make you feel discouraged and cause you to lose hope in your recovery. One way to fight self-stigma is to educate yourself about psychiatric symptoms and mental disorders, and to be able to separate myths from facts. For example, knowing that no one causes schizophrenia can help you to stop blaming yourself or others.

Another way to fight self-stigma is to belong to a support group or another group where you get to know different people who have experienced psychiatric symptoms. You can locate support groups through organizations such as the Consumer Organization and Networking Technical Assistance Center (CONTAC) and the National Empowerment Center. Contact information is provided for these and other helpful organizations in the Appendix to the "Recovery Strategies" handout.

> *The more you know about mental disorders, the more you can combat prejudice, whether it comes from others or from within yourself.*

Correct misinformation in others without disclosing anything about your own experience.

A co-worker might say, "People with mental illness are all dangerous." You might decide to reply, "Actually, I read a long article in the paper that said that the majority of people with mental illness are not violent. The media just sensationalizes certain cases."

> *To fight stigma, you might decide to correct misinformation without disclosing personal experience.*

Selectively disclose your experience with psychiatric symptoms.

Disclosing information about your own experience with psychiatric symptoms is a personal decision. It's important to think about how the other person might respond. It's also important to weigh the risks and benefits to yourself, both in the short term and in the long term. Talking this over with someone in your support system might be helpful.

People vary widely in whether they choose to disclose information about themselves, and if so, how much. You may decide to disclose personal information only to family members or close friends. Or you may disclose information to people only when it becomes necessary. For example, you might need a specific accommodation in order to perform your job.

You may feel comfortable disclosing information in a wide variety of settings. You may even be willing to speak publicly about mental illness for educational or advocacy purposes.

In certain situations, you might decide to fight stigma by disclosing some of your own experience.

Become aware of your legal rights

It's important to educate yourself about the laws against discrimination. Two major laws that protect against unfair treatment are the Americans with Disabilities Act (ADA) and the Fair Housing Act (FHA).

The Americans with Disabilities Act makes it illegal to discriminate against people with physical or psychiatric disabilities in employment, transportation, communication, or recreation. The Fair Housing Act prohibits housing discrimination because of race, color, national origin, religion, sex, family status, or disability (physical or psychiatric).

It is worthwhile to take some time to understand the basic principles of these laws and how they might apply to you. If you feel that your legal rights have been violated, there is a range of possible actions you might take, depending on the situation.

Sometimes it is most effective to speak directly to the person involved. For example, it is usually preferable to approach your employer about the need to provide a reasonable accommodation on the job. An example of a reasonable accommodation would be asking to move your desk to a more quiet area in the office to improve your concentration.

Sometimes it may be more effective to talk to an expert to get advice, support, advocacy, mediation, and even legal help. For example, if a landlord refused to rent you an apartment because of psychiatric symptoms you may need to contact the Office of Fair Housing and Equal Opportunity

(FHEO) in the Department of Housing and Urban Development (HUD) for advice and assistance. If an employer was unresponsive to your request for accommodation on the job, you might want to contact the Equal Employment Opportunity Commission (EEOC).

Contact information for the Office of Fair Housing and Equal Opportunity, the Equal Employment Opportunity Commission and other helpful organizations is provided at the end of this Appendix.

> *To combat stigma, it is important to know your legal rights and where to seek help if your rights have been violated.*

Question: What strategies have you used to combat stigma?
You can use the following checklist to answer this question.

Strategies for Combating Stigma

Strategy	I have used this strategy
Educating yourself about psychiatric symptoms and mental disorders	
Correcting misinformation without disclosing your own experience with psychiatric symptoms	
Selectively disclosing your experience with psychiatric symptoms	
Becoming aware of your legal rights	
Seeking out assistance if your legal rights are violated	
Other Strategies:	

Facts About Bipolar Disorder

CHAPTER 2B

Introduction

This handout provides information about bipolar disorder. Facts are given about how a diagnosis is made, the symptoms, how common it is, and the possible courses of the disorder. Several examples are included of famous people who have experienced the symptoms of bipolar disorder and have made positive contributions to society.

What is bipolar disorder?

Bipolar disorder is a major mental illness that affects many people. It is sometimes called "manic depression." About one person in every one hundred people (1%) develops the disorder at some time in his or her life. It occurs in every country, every culture, every racial group and at every income level.

Bipolar disorder causes symptoms that can interfere with many aspects of people's lives. Some of the symptoms cause severe mood swings, from the highest of highs (mania) to the lowest of the lows (depression.) Some of the other symptoms of bipolar disorder can make it difficult to know what's real and what's not real (psychotic symptoms).

It is important to know that there are many reasons to be optimistic about the future:

- There is effective treatment for bipolar disorder.
- People with bipolar disorder can learn to manage their illness.

- People with bipolar disorder can lead productive lives.

The more you understand about the illness and take an active role in your treatment, the better you will feel and the more you can accomplish toward your life goals.

Bipolar disorder is a major mental illness that affects many aspects of a person's life.

1 in every 100 people develops bipolar disorder at some point in his or her life.

People can learn to manage the symptoms of bipolar disorder and lead productive lives.

Question: What did you know about bipolar disorder before you had personal experience with it?

How is bipolar disorder diagnosed?

Bipolar disorder is diagnosed based on a clinical interview conducted by a specially trained professional, usually a doctor, but sometimes a nurse, psychologist, social worker or other mental health practitioner. In the interview, there are questions about symptoms you have experienced and how you are functioning in different areas of your life, such as relationships and work.

There is currently no blood test, X-ray or brain scan that can be used to diagnose bipolar disorder. To make an accurate diagnosis, however, the doctor may also request a physical exam and certain lab tests or blood tests in order to rule out other causes of symptoms, such as a brain tumor or an injury to the brain.

> *Bipolar disorder is diagnosed by a clinical interview with a mental health professional.*

Question: How long did it take for a mental health professional to accurately diagnose the symptoms you experienced?

What are the symptoms of bipolar disorder?

It is important to keep in mind that the symptoms of bipolar disorder can be found in other mental disorders. Specifying a diagnosis of bipolar disorder is based on a combination of different symptoms, how long they have been present, and their severity. Symptoms that occur only when a person has used alcohol or drugs are not included.

No one has the exact same symptoms or is bothered to the same degree. You may, however, recognize having experienced some of the following symptoms:

Extremely high moods are called "mania."

People who have had periods of mania have reported the following symptoms:

Feelings of extreme happiness or excitement. "I was so happy with my life; I felt like I was on top of the world. I thought the whole world loved me and worshipped me."

Feeling irritable. "I thought I had a brilliant plan for making thousands of dollars. I got very irritated when people asked questions that seemed to doubt me."

Feeling unrealistically self-confident. "I sent a hand written script to Steven Speilberg. I was absolutely sure that he would buy it immediately for his next movie."

Sleeping less. "I felt like I only needed two hours of sleep a night. I was too excited to sleep any more than that."

Talking a lot. "People told me I was talking all the time; they couldn't get a word in edgewise. I couldn't seem to stop myself because I had so much to say."

Having racing thoughts. "My head was so full of thoughts I couldn't keep up with them."

Being easily distracted. "I couldn't concentrate on what my English teacher was saying because I was distracted by every other sound—the ticking of the clock, the air conditioner humming, a car driving by, someone walking by in the hall, a bird singing outside the window. It was overwhelming."

Being extremely active. "Sometimes I would work 20 hours a day on my inventions. Or I would re-arrange every stick of furniture in my house—then change it again the next day."

Having bad judgment. "I thought nothing bad could happen to me, so I spent everything in my bank account, borrowed from everyone I knew, then ran up all my charge cards. I also had a one night stand with someone that I didn't know at all—I was lucky he didn't have AIDS or something."

Extremely low moods are called "depression."

"Depression" is defined as including:

Sad mood. "I couldn't see anything positive in my life. Everything seemed dark and negative."

Eating too little or too much. "When I am depressed, I lost all interest in food. Nothing looks good and I hardly eat anything. I lost ten pounds the last time."

Sleeping too little or too much. "I had a lot of trouble falling sleep at night. I would lay awake for hours, tossing and turning. Then I would wake up at 4:00 AM and not be able to go back to sleep. Other people I know with depression have the opposite problem. They feel like sleeping all the time—they spend 12 or more hours a day in bed."

Feeling tired and low energy. "I dragged myself to work each morning, but I could barely answer the phone once I got there. Everything seemed like such an effort."

Feeling helpless, hopeless, worthless. "I broke up with my boyfriend because I thought I was a loser and he shouldn't be stuck with me. He deserved better. It seemed like nothing I did turned out right. I saw nothing but heartache in my future."

Feeling guilty for things that aren't your fault. "I started feeling responsible for all kinds of things: my brother's having cerebral palsy, the car accident that happened in front of my house, even the hurricane that blew the roofs off the buildings down in Florida. Somehow I thought it was all my fault."

Suicidal thoughts or actions. "When I reached the bottom, I felt that the only way out was to leave this world. I thought my wife and kids would be better off without me. Luckily I didn't do anything to hurt myself, although I considered it."

Trouble concentrating and making decisions. "It took me over an hour to read a one page letter from my bank. I couldn't keep my mind focused. And one day I couldn't go to work because I couldn't decide what shirt to wear."

Symptoms that make it hard to know what's real are called "psychotic symptoms."

Some people with bipolar disorder have psychotic symptoms. They have described the following experiences:

Hearing, seeing, feeling or smelling something that is not actually there ("hallucinations"). "I heard different kinds of voices. Sometimes the voices were o.k., just making comments like 'now you're eating lunch.' But sometimes the voices said things like 'you're stupid; no one wants to be friends with such a loser.' Or they might say scary things about other people, 'he has a knife and wants to kill you.'"

Having very unusual or unrealistic beliefs that are not shared by others in your culture or religion ("delusions"). "I was convinced that I had special mental powers that could stop missiles in their tracks. I thought the FBI was after me because they wanted to control these powers. I even thought the TV was talking about this."

Confused thinking ("thought disorder.") "I used to try to tell my sister what I was thinking, but I would jump from topic to topic and she told me she had no idea what I was talking about."

The major symptoms of bipolar disorder are mania, depression, and psychotic symptoms.

No one has exactly the same symptoms or experiences them to the same degree.

Question: Which of the symptoms have you experienced? You can use the following checklists to record your answer.

Symptoms of Mania

Symptom of Mania	I had this symptom	Example
Feeling extremely happy or excited		
Feeling irritable		
Feeling unrealistically self confident		
Sleeping less		
Talking a lot		
Having racing thoughts		
Being easily distracted		
Being extremely active		
Having faulty judgment		

Symptoms of Depression

Symptom of depression	I had this symptom	example
Sad mood		
Eating too little or too much		
Sleeping too little or too much		
Feeling tired and low energy		
Feeling helpless, hopeless, worthless		
Feeling guilty for things that weren't my fault		
Suicidal thoughts or actions		
Trouble concentrating & making decisions		

Symptoms of Psychosis

Symptom of psychosis	I had this symptom	Example
Hearing, seeing, feeling or smelling something that is not actually present		
Confused thinking		
Having very unusual or unrealistic beliefs that are not shared by others in my culture		

What causes bipolar disorder?

Bipolar disorder is nobody's fault. This means that you did not cause the disorder and neither did your family members or anyone else. Scientists believe that the symptoms of bipolar disorder are caused by a chemical imbalance in the brain. Chemicals called "neurotransmitters" send messages in the brain. When they are out of balance, they can cause extreme shifts in your mood. This chemical imbalance can also cause the brain to send messages that contain wrong information.

Scientists do not know what causes this chemical imbalance, but they believe that whatever causes it happens before birth. This means that people have a "biological vulnerability" to develop bipolar disorder, which then develops at a later age.

In addition to biological vulnerability, stress is also believed to play a role in the onset and course of bipolar disorder. The theory of how vulnerability and stress interact with each other is called the "stress-vulnerability model" and is covered in more detail in the handout "The Stress-Vulnerability Model and Treatment Strategies."

Many questions about bipolar disorder remain unanswered. There are many research projects underway to try to learn more about the illness.

> *Bipolar disorder is nobody's fault.*

> *Scientists believe that bipolar disorder is caused by a chemical imbalance in the brain.*

<u>Question</u>: What other explanations have you heard about what causes bipolar disorder?

What is the course of bipolar disorder?
What happens after you first develop symptoms?

People usually develop bipolar disorders as teenagers or young adults, approximately age 16 to age 30. People can also have their first symptoms when they are in their 40's or 50's. People vary in how often they have symptoms, the severity of the symptoms and how much the disorder interferes with their lives.

Bipolar disorder affects people in very different ways. Some people have a milder form of the disorder and only have symptoms a few times in their lives. Other people have a stronger form of the disorder and have several episodes, some of which require hospitalization.

Bipolar tends to be episodic, with symptoms varying in intensity over time. When symptoms reappear or get worse, this is usually referred to as a "symptom exacerbation" or an "acute episode" or a "relapse." (More information on this subject is provided in the handout, "Reducing Relapses.") Some relapses can be managed at home, but other relapses may require hospitalization to protect the person or others.

With effective treatment, most people with bipolar disorder can reduce their symptoms and live productive, meaningful lives.

> *Bipolar disorder tends to be episodic, with symptoms coming and going at varying levels of intensity.*

Question: What has been your experience with symptom relapses?

Examples of people who have bipolar disorder

Some famous people have developed bipolar disorder:

Patti Duke is an American actress who had her own television series and has starred in movies, including "The Miracle Worker." She also had a singing and writing career.

Robert Boorstin was a special assistant to President Clinton. His work was highly valued in the White House.

Vincent Van Gogh was one of the most famous painters who ever lived.

Kay Redfield Jamison is a psychologist, researcher and writer. In 2001 she won a MacArthur Fellowship, sometimes referred to as " the genius award."

Other people who have developed bipolar disorder are not famous, but are quietly leading productive, creative, meaningful lives:

Ms. X is an attorney in a large law firm and is active in her church.

Mr. Y teaches in an elementary school. He is married and is expecting his first child.

Mr. Z is actively looking for work. He used to need frequent hospitalizations, but has successfully stayed out of the hospital for 3 years.

> *There are countless positive examples of people with bipolar disorder who have contributed to society.*

Questions: Do you know other people with bipolar disorder?
If so, what are some examples of their personal strengths?

What is stigma?

When referring to mental illness, the word "stigma" means the negative opinions and attitudes that some people have about mental illness. Not everyone with mental illness has experienced stigma, although unfortunately, many have.

It is important to know that there are two major laws that protect against discrimination against people with physical or psychiatric disabilities. The Americans with Disabilities Act (ADA) makes it illegal to discriminate in the areas of employment, transportation, communication or recreation. The Fair Housing Act (FHA) prohibits housing discrimination.

Stigma is a complicated problem, and there are no easy solutions. Research has shown that as the general public gets to know more about mental disorders and as they get to know people who have experienced psychiatric symptoms, their negative beliefs go down.

Many organizations, including the National Institute of Mental Health, the Center for Mental Health Services, the National Alliance for the Mentally Ill, the National Mental Health Association, and the National Empowerment Center, are working on national campaigns to educate the public and create more laws that protect against discrimination. Contact information for these organizations is listed in the Appendix of the "Recovery Strategies" handout.

If you have experienced stigma and/or would like to know more about strategies for responding to stigma, refer to the Appendix at the end of this handout.

> *Stigma refers to negative opinions and attitudes about mental illness.*

Question: Have you ever experienced stigma because of psychiatric symptoms?

What are some of the steps you can take to manage your illness?

By reading this handout you are already taking an important step, which is learning some practical facts about your illness.

Other important steps include:

- Learning how to cope with stress
- Building social support
- Developing a relapse prevention plan
- Using medication effectively
- Learning how to cope with symptoms
- Getting your needs met in the mental health system

These steps will be covered in the other educational handouts in the Illness Management and Recovery Program.

What you do makes a difference in your recovery.

There are steps you can take to manage psychiatric symptoms effectively.

Summary of the main points about bipolar disorder:

- *Bipolar disorder is a major psychiatric disorder that affects many aspects of a person's life.*

- *1 in every 100 people develops bipolar disorder at some point in his or her life.*

- *People can learn to manage the symptoms of bipolar disorder and lead productive lives.*

- *Bipolar disorder is diagnosed by a clinical interview with a mental health professional.*

- *The major symptoms of bipolar disorder are mania, depression, and psychotic symptoms.*

- *No one has exactly the same symptoms or experiences them to the same degree.*

- *Bipolar disorder is nobody's fault.*

- *Scientists believe that bipolar disorder is caused by a chemical imbalance in the brain.*

- *Bipolar disorder tends to be episodic, with symptoms coming and going at varying levels of intensity.*

- *There are countless positive examples of people with bipolar disorder who have contributed to society.*

- *Stigma refers to negative opinions and attitudes about mental illness.*

- *What you do makes a difference in your recovery.*

- *There are steps you can take to manage psychiatric symptoms effectively.*

Appendix: Strategies and Resources for Responding to Stigma

What are some strategies for responding to stigma?

It may be helpful for you to develop some personal strategies for responding to stigma. There are advantages and disadvantages to each strategy. What you decide to do depends on the specific situation.

Some possible strategies include:

Educate yourself about mental disorders

Sometimes people who experience psychiatric symptoms do not know the facts themselves. They may blame themselves for their symptoms or think they cannot take care of themselves or that they can't be part of the community. You may have had these negative thoughts or feelings. This is called "self-stigma."

It is important to fight self-stigma, because it can make you feel discouraged and cause you to lose hope in your recovery. One way to fight self-stigma is to educate yourself about psychiatric symptoms and mental disorders, and to be able to separate myths from facts. For example, knowing that no one causes bipolar disorder can help you to stop blaming yourself or others.

Another way to fight self-stigma is to belong to a support group or another group where you get to know different people who have experienced psychiatric symptoms. You can locate support groups through organizations such as the Consumer Organization and Networking Technical Assistance Center (CONTAC) and the National Empowerment Center. Contact information is provided for these and other helpful organizations in the Appendix to the "Recovery Strategies" handout.

> *The more you know about mental disorders, the more you can combat prejudice, whether it comes from others or from within yourself.*

Correct misinformation in others without disclosing anything about your own experience.

A co-worker might say, "People with mental illness are all dangerous." You might decide to reply, "Actually, I read a long article in the paper that said that the majority of people with mental illness are not violent. The media just sensationalizes certain cases."

> *To fight stigma, you might decide to correct misinformation without disclosing personal experience.*

Selectively disclose your experience with psychiatric symptoms.

Disclosing information about your own experience with psychiatric symptoms is a personal decision. It's important to think about how the other person might respond. It's also important to weigh the risks and benefits to yourself, both in the short term and in the long term. Talking this over with someone in your support system might be helpful.

People vary widely in whether they choose to disclose information about themselves, and if so, how much. You may decide to disclose personal information only to family members or close friends. Or you may disclose information to people only when it becomes necessary. For example, you might need a specific accommodation in order to perform your job.

You may feel comfortable disclosing information in a wide variety of settings. You may even be willing to speak publicly about mental illness for educational or advocacy purposes.

In certain situations, you might decide to fight stigma by disclosing some of your own experience.

Become aware of your legal rights

It's important to educate yourself about the laws against discrimination. Two major laws that protect against unfair treatment are the Americans with Disabilities Act (ADA) and the Fair Housing Act (FHA).

The Americans with Disabilities Act makes it illegal to discriminate against people with physical or psychiatric disabilities in employment, transportation, communication, or recreation. The Fair Housing Act prohibits housing discrimination because of race, color, national origin, religion, sex, family status, or disability (physical or psychiatric).

It is worthwhile to take some time to understand the basic principles of these laws and how they might apply to you. If you feel that your legal rights have been violated, there is a range of possible actions you might take, depending on the situation.

Sometimes it is most effective to speak directly to the person involved. For example, it is usually preferable to approach your employer about the need to provide a reasonable accommodation on the job. An example of a reasonable accommodation would be asking to move your desk to a more quiet area in the office to improve your concentration.

Sometimes it may be more effective to talk to an expert to get advice, support, advocacy, mediation, and even legal help. For example, if a landlord refused to rent you an apartment because of psychiatric symptoms you may need to contact the Office of Fair Housing and Equal Opportunity

(FHEO) in the Department of Housing and Urban Development (HUD) for advice and assistance. If an employer was unresponsive to your request for accommodation on the job, you might want to contact the Equal Employment Opportunity Commission (EEOC).

Contact information for the Office of Fair Housing and Equal Opportunity, the Equal Employment Opportunity Commission and other helpful organizations is provided at the end of this Appendix.

> *To combat stigma, it is important to know your legal rights and where to seek help if your rights have been violated.*

Question: What strategies have you used to combat stigma?
You can use the following checklist to answer this question.

Strategies for Combating Stigma

Strategy	I have used this strategy
Educating yourself about psychiatric symptoms and mental disorders	
Correcting misinformation without disclosing your own experience with psychiatric symptoms	
Selectively disclosing your experience with psychiatric symptoms	
Becoming aware of your legal rights	
Seeking out assistance if your legal rights are violated	
Other Strategies:	

Facts About Depression

CHAPTER 2C

Introduction

This handout provides information about the psychiatric disorder of depression, focusing on the diagnosis of major depression. Facts are given about how a diagnosis is made, the symptoms, how common it is, and the possible courses of the disorder. Several examples are included of famous people who have experienced symptoms of depression and have made positive contributions to society.

What is depression?

Depression is one of the most common psychiatric disorders. 15 to 20 people out of every 100 have a period of serious depression at some time in their lives. It occurs in every country, every culture, every racial group and at every income level.

Depression causes people to have extremely low moods, when they feel very sad or "blue." It can also cause problems in appetite, sleeping and energy level. For some people, depression can seriously interfere with their work and social life.

It is important to know that there are many reasons to be optimistic about the future:

- There is effective treatment for depression
- People with depression can learn to manage their own illness
- People with depression can lead productive lives.

The more you understand about the illness and take an active role in your treatment, the better you will feel and the more you can accomplish toward your life goals.

> *Depression is a major mental illness that can affect many aspects of a person's life.*

> *15 to 20 people in every 100 have a period of serious depression at some time in their lives.*

> *People can learn to manage the symptoms of depression and lead productive lives.*

Question: What did you know about depression before you had personal experience with it?

How is depression diagnosed?

Depression is diagnosed based on a clinical interview conducted by a specially trained professional, usually a doctor, but sometimes a nurse, psychologist, social worker or other mental health practitioner. In the interview, there are questions about symptoms you have experienced and how you are functioning in different areas of your life, such as relationships and work.

There is currently no blood test, X-ray or brain scan that can be used to diagnose depression. To make an accurate diagnosis, however, the doctor may also request a physical exam and certain lab tests or blood tests in order to rule out other causes of symptoms, such as a thyroid problem.

Depression is diagnosed by a clinical interview with a mental health professional.

Question: How long did it take for a mental health professional to accurately diagnose the symptoms you experienced?

What are the symptoms of depression?

It is important to keep in mind that the symptoms of depression can be found in other mental disorders. Specifying a diagnosis of depression is based on a combination of different symptoms, how long they have been present, and their severity. Symptoms that occur only when a person has used alcohol or drugs are not included

It is also important to recognize that there are different levels of severity of depression. This handout focuses on the diagnosis of "major depressive disorder." This diagnosis includes having one or more episodes of at least two weeks in which there is an extremely depressed (sad) mood or the loss of interest or pleasure in nearly all activities. To receive a diagnosis of major depression, there are several other additional symptoms that must be present at the same time, such as changes in appetite, sleep, energy, and concentration.

No one has the exact same symptoms or is bothered to the same degree. If you have major depression, however, you may recognize having experienced some of the following symptoms:

<u>Sad mood</u>. "I couldn't see anything positive in my life. Everything seemed dark and negative. I felt down all the time."

<u>Eating too little or too much</u>. "When I'm depressed I lose all interest in food. Nothing tastes good and I hardly eat anything. Last time I lost ten pounds."

<u>Sleeping too little or too much.</u> "I had a lot of trouble falling sleep at night. I would lay awake for hours, tossing and turning. Then I would wake up at 4:00 AM and not be able to go back to sleep. Other people I know with depression have the opposite problem. They feel like sleeping all the time—they spend 12 or more hours a day in bed."

<u>Feeling tired and low energy</u>. "I dragged myself to work each morning, but I could barely answer the phone once I got there. Everything seemed like too much effort."

<u>Feeling helpless, hopeless, worthless</u>. "I broke up with my boyfriend because I thought I was a loser and he shouldn't be stuck with me. He deserved better. It seemed like nothing I did turned out right. I saw nothing but heartache in my future."

<u>Feeling guilty for things that aren't your fault.</u> "I started feeling responsible for all kinds of things: my brother's having cerebral palsy, the car accident that happened in front of my house, even the hurricane that blew the roofs off the buildings down in Florida. Somehow I thought it was all my fault."

<u>Suicidal thoughts or actions</u>. "When I reached the bottom, I felt that the only way out was to leave this world. I thought my wife and kids would be better off without me. Luckily I didn't do anything to hurt myself, although I considered it."

<u>Trouble concentrating and making decisions.</u> "It took me over an hour to read a one page letter from my bank. I couldn't keep my mind focused. And one day I couldn't go to work because I couldn't decide what shirt to wear."

The major symptoms of depression include:
- *Sad mood*
- *Eating too little or too much*
- *Sleeping too little or too much*
- *Feeling tired or low energy*
- *Feeling helpless, hopeless, or worthless*
- *Feeling guilty for things that aren't your fault*
- *Suicidal thoughts or actions*
- *Trouble concentrating and making decisions*

No one has exactly the same symptoms or experiences them to the same degree.

<u>Question:</u> Which of the symptoms have you experienced? You can use the following checklist to record your answers.

Symptoms of Depression

Symptom of depression	I had this symptom	example
Sad mood		
Eating too little or too much		
Sleeping too little or too much		
Feeling tired and low energy		
Feeling helpless, hopeless, worthless		
Feeling guilty for things that weren't my fault		
Suicidal thoughts or actions		
Trouble concentrating & making decisions		

What causes depression?

It is extremely important to know that depression is not your fault. Sometimes when people are depressed they start to think that they caused it. This is not true. Scientists believe that the symptoms of depression are caused by a chemical imbalance in the brain. Chemicals called "neurotransmitters" send messages in the brain. When these chemicals are out of balance, they can cause low moods.

Research has found that the experience of a major stress or loss, such as losing a loved one, or being the victim of abuse or violence, can increase the chances of a person developing depression. Stress also appears to play a role in the course of depression. The theory of how biological vulnerability and stress interact with each other is called the "stress-vulnerability model" and is covered in more detail in the handout "The Stress-Vulnerability Model and Treatment Strategies."

Many questions about depression remain unanswered. There are many research projects underway to try to learn more about the disorder.

> *Depression is not your fault.*

> *Scientists believe that the symptoms of depression are caused by a chemical imbalance in the brain.*

Question: What other explanations have you heard about what causes depression?

What is the course of depression? What happens after you first develop symptoms?

People can develop depression at any time in their lives. People vary in how often they have symptoms, the severity of the symptoms and how much the disorder interferes with their lives. Some people only have symptoms a few times in their lives. Other people have several episodes, some of which may require hospitalization.

Depression tends to be episodic, with symptoms varying in intensity over time. When symptoms reappear or get worse, this is usually referred to as a "relapse," or "acute episode" or "symptoms exacerbation." (More information on this subject is provided in the handout, "Reducing Relapses.") Some relapses can be managed at home, but other relapses may require hospitalization to protect the person.

With effective treatment, most people with depression can reduce their symptoms and live productive, meaningful lives.

> *Depression tends to be episodic, with symptoms coming and going at varying levels of intensity.*

Question: What has been your experience with symptom relapses?

Examples of people who have depression

Some famous people have been troubled by depression:

Winston Churchill was the Prime Minister of England during World War II and led his country to victory.

Mike Wallace is an American television journalist, well known for conducting interviews on the show "60 Minutes."

Other people who have developed depression are not famous, but are quietly leading productive, creative, meaningful lives:

Mr. Y is a college student who plays on the soccer team.

Ms. Z is married and the mother of a 2-year-old son. She works at home and cares for her child.

There are countless positive examples of people with depression who have contributed to society.

Questions: Do you know other people with depression?
If so, what are some examples of their personal strengths?

What is stigma?

When referring to mental illness, the word "stigma" means the negative opinions and attitudes that some people have about mental illness. Not everyone with mental illness has experienced stigma, although unfortunately, many have.

It is important to know that there are two major laws that protect against discrimination against people with physical or psychiatric disabilities. The Americans with Disabilities Act (ADA) makes it illegal to discriminate in the areas of employment, transportation, communication or recreation. The Fair Housing Act (FHA) prohibits housing discrimination.

Stigma is a complicated problem, and there are no easy solutions. Research has shown that as the general public gets to know more about mental disorders and as they get to know people who have experienced psychiatric symptoms, their negative beliefs go down.

Many organizations, including the National Institute of Mental Health, the Center for Mental Health Services, the National Alliance for the Mentally Ill, the National Mental Health Association, and the National Empowerment Center, are working on national campaigns to educate the public and create more laws that protect against discrimination. Contact information for these organizations is listed in the Appendix of the "Recovery Strategies" handout.

If you have experienced stigma and/or would like to know more about strategies for responding to stigma, refer to the Appendix at the end of this handout.

> *Stigma refers to negative opinions and attitudes about mental illness.*

<u>Question</u>:   Have you ever experienced stigma because of psychiatric symptoms?

What are some of the steps you can take to manage your illness?

By reading this module you are already taking the first step, which is learning some practical facts about your illness.

Other important steps include:

- Learning how to cope with stress
- Building social support
- Developing a relapse prevention plan
- Using medication effectively
- Learning how to cope with symptoms
- Getting your needs met in the mental health system

These steps will be covered in the other educational handouts in the Illness Management and Recovery Program.

What you do makes a difference in your recovery.

There are steps you can take to manage psychiatric symptoms effectively.

Summary of the main points about depression:

- *Depression is a major psychiatric disorder that affects many aspects of a person's life.*

- *15 to 20 people in every 100 have a period of serious depression at some time in their lives.*

- *People can learn to manage the symptoms of depression and lead productive lives.*

- *Depression is diagnosed by a clinical interview with a mental health professional.*

- *The symptoms of depression include:*
    - *Sad mood*
    - *Eating too little or too much*
    - *Sleeping too little or too much*
    - *Feeling tired or low energy*
    - *Feeling helpless, hopeless, or worthless*
    - *Feeling guilty for things that aren't your fault*
    - *Suicidal thoughts or actions*
    - *Trouble concentrating and making decisions*

- *No one has exactly the same symptoms or experiences them to the same degree.*

- *Depression is not your fault.*

- *Scientists believe that depression is caused by a chemical imbalance in the brain.*

- *Depression tends to be episodic, with symptoms coming and going at varying levels of intensity.*

- *There are countless positive examples of people with depression who have contributed to society.*

- *Stigma refers to negative opinions and attitudes about mental illness.*

- *What you do makes a difference in your recovery.*

- *There are steps you can take to manage psychiatric symptoms effectively.*

Appendix: Strategies and Resources for Responding to Stigma

What are some strategies for responding to stigma?

It may be helpful for you to develop some personal strategies for responding to stigma. There are advantages and disadvantages to each strategy. What you decide to do depends on the specific situation.

Some possible strategies include:

Educate yourself about mental disorders

Sometimes people who experience psychiatric symptoms do not know the facts themselves. They may blame themselves for their symptoms or think they cannot take care of themselves or that they can't be part of the community. You may have had these negative thoughts or feelings. This is called "self-stigma."

It is important to fight self-stigma, because it can make you feel discouraged and cause you to lose hope in your recovery. One way to fight self-stigma is to educate yourself about psychiatric symptoms and mental disorders, and to be able to separate myths from facts. For example, knowing that you did not cause your depression can help you to stop blaming yourself.

Another way to fight self-stigma is to belong to a support group or another group where you get to know different people who have experienced psychiatric symptoms. You can locate support groups through organizations such as the Consumer Organization and Networking Technical Assistance Center (CONTAC) and the National Empowerment Center. Contact information is provided for these and other helpful organizations in the Appendix to the "Recovery Strategies" handout.

> *The more you know about mental disorders, the more you can combat prejudice, whether it comes from others or from within yourself.*

Correct misinformation in others without disclosing anything about your own experience.

A co-worker might say, "People with mental illness are all dangerous." You might decide to reply, "Actually, I read a long article in the paper that said that the majority of people with mental illness are not violent. The media just sensationalizes certain cases."

> *To fight stigma, you might decide to correct misinformation without disclosing personal experience.*

Selectively disclose your experience with psychiatric symptoms.

Disclosing information about your own experience with psychiatric symptoms is a personal decision. It's important to think about how the other person might respond. It's also important to weigh the risks and benefits to yourself, both in the short term and in the long term. Talking this over with someone in your support system might be helpful.

People vary widely in whether they choose to disclose information about themselves, and if so, how much. You may decide to disclose personal information only to family members or close friends. Or you may disclose information to people only when it becomes necessary. For example, you might need a specific accommodation in order to perform your job.

You may feel comfortable disclosing information in a wide variety of settings. You may even be willing to speak publicly about mental illness for educational or advocacy purposes.

In certain situations, you might decide to fight stigma by disclosing some of your own experience.

Become aware of your legal rights

It's important to educate yourself about the laws against discrimination. Two major laws that protect against unfair treatment are the Americans with Disabilities Act (ADA) and the Fair Housing Act (FHA).

The Americans with Disabilities Act makes it illegal to discriminate against people with physical or psychiatric disabilities in employment, transportation, communication, or recreation. The Fair Housing Act prohibits housing discrimination because of race, color, national origin, religion, sex, family status, or disability (physical or psychiatric).

It is worthwhile to take some time to understand the basic principles of these laws and how they might apply to you. If you feel that your legal rights have been violated, there is a range of possible actions you might take, depending on the situation.

Sometimes it is most effective to speak directly to the person involved. For example, it is usually preferable to approach your employer about the need to provide a reasonable accommodation on the job. An example of a reasonable accommodation would be asking to move your desk to a more quiet area in the office to improve your concentration.

Sometimes it may be more effective to talk to an expert to get advice, support, advocacy, mediation, and even legal help. For example, if a landlord refused to rent you an apartment because of psychiatric symptoms you may need to contact the Office of Fair Housing and Equal Opportunity

(FHEO) in the Department of Housing and Urban Development (HUD) for advice and assistance. If an employer was unresponsive to your request for accommodation on the job, you might want to contact the Equal Employment Opportunity Commission (EEOC).

Contact information for the Office of Fair Housing and Equal Opportunity, the Equal Employment Opportunity Commission and other helpful organizations is provided at the end of this Appendix.

> *To combat stigma, it is important to know your legal rights and where to seek help if your rights have been violated.*

Question: What strategies have you used to combat stigma?
You can use the following checklist to answer this question.

Strategies for Combating Stigma

Strategy	I have used this strategy
Educating yourself about psychiatric symptoms and mental disorders	
Correcting misinformation without disclosing your own experience with psychiatric symptoms	
Selectively disclosing your experience with psychiatric symptoms	
Becoming aware of your legal rights	
Seeking out assistance if your legal rights are violated	
Other Strategies:	

Stress Model and Treatment Strategies

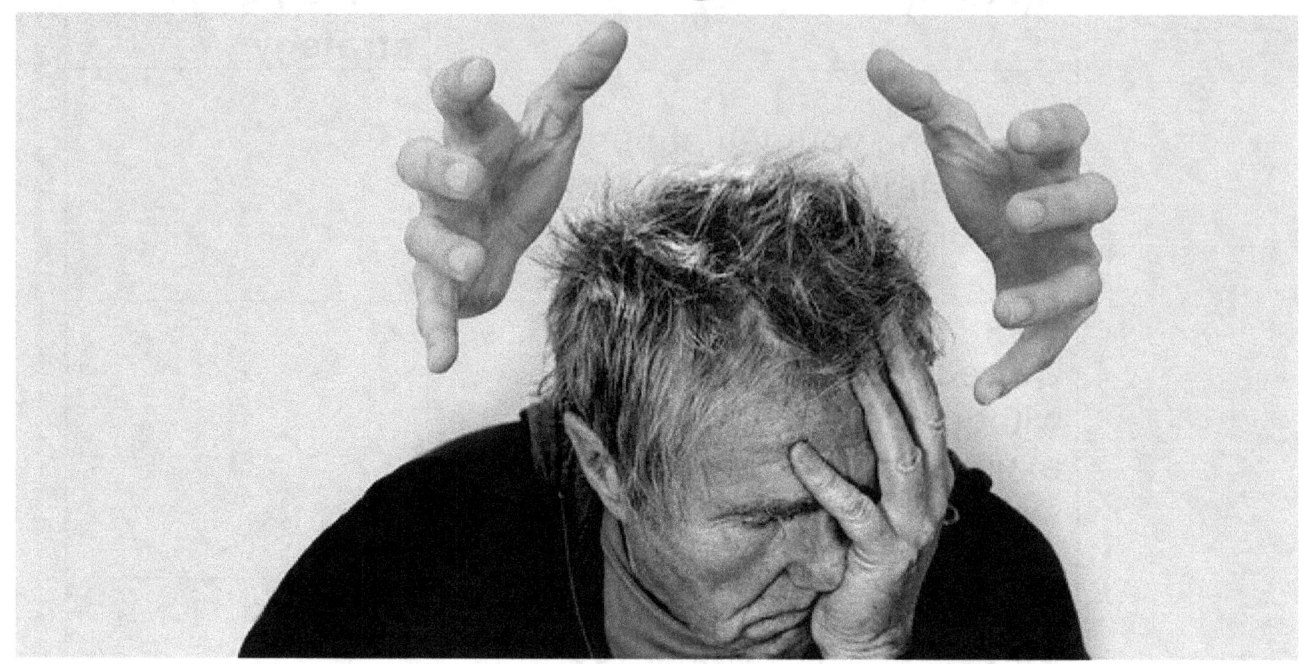

CHAPTER 3

Introduction

This handout describes a model for understanding the nature of psychiatric disorders, including factors which can influence the course of these disorders. According to this model, the stress-vulnerability model, psychiatric illnesses have a biological basis. This biological basis or vulnerability can be made worse by stress and substance use, but can be improved by medication and by leading a healthy lifestyle.

The stress-vulnerability model can help you understand what influences your disorder and how you can minimize the effects of the disorder on your life.

Appendix 1 contains a diagram which summarizes the stress-vulnerability model. The components of the diagram are described in detail in this handout.

What causes psychiatric symptoms?

Scientists do not yet understand exactly why some people have symptoms of mental illness and others do not. They also cannot predict who will have several episodes of symptoms and who will have one or only a few. One theory that has received strong support is called the "stress-vulnerability model." According to this theory, both stress and biological vulnerability contribute to symptoms.

> *Both stress and biology contribute to symptoms.*

What are the biological factors in mental illness?

The term "biological vulnerability" refers to people who are born with, or who acquire very early in life, a tendency to develop a problem in a specific medical area. For example, some people have a biological vulnerability to developing asthma, and other people have a biological vulnerability to developing high blood pressure or diabetes. Similarly, it is thought that people can have biological vulnerabilities to develop schizophrenia, bipolar disorder, or depression.

In diabetes, the part of the body that is affected is the pancreas, which keeps the level of insulin in balance. In mental illness, the part of the body that is affected is the brain, which is made up of billions of nerve cells (neurons) containing different chemicals (neurotransmitters). Scientists believe that mental illnesses are caused by imbalances in these neurotransmitters in the brain.

As with other disorders, such as diabetes, hypertension, and heart disease, genetic factors play a role in the vulnerability to mental illness. The chances of a person developing depression, bipolar disorder, or schizophrenia are higher if a close relative also has the disorder. Many scientific studies, including the international human genome project, are researching the genetic factors related to mental illness

Genetic factors, however, do not explain everything about why some people develop mental illness. For example, for many people with mental illness, there is no history of anyone else in their family who experienced psychiatric symptoms. It is widely believed that non-genetic factors may also contribute to people developing mental illnesses. For example, early biological factors, such as exposure to a virus when the baby is in the womb, may be important.

There is little scientific evidence that alcohol use or drug use causes people to develop a biological vulnerability to mental illness in the first place. However, when someone already has a biological vulnerability, alcohol and drug use may trigger symptoms or make them worse.

> *Biology plays a part in whether someone is vulnerable to developing a mental illness.*

> *Biological factors contribute to the chemical imbalance in the brain that scientists have associated with psychiatric symptoms.*

Questions: Are you aware of any of your family members who have had (or might have had) a mental illness?
Have you had experience with alcohol or drugs that seemed to make your symptoms more severe?

What are the stress factors in mental illness?

Scientists believe that stress also plays an important part in psychiatric symptoms. Stress can trigger the onset of symptoms or make them worse. Stress may play a particularly strong role in increasing the biological vulnerability to depression. For example, if someone has lost a loved one, been the victim of a sexual or physical assault, witnessed a tragic event or experienced other examples of extraordinary stressors, he or she may be more likely to become depressed.

How people experience stress is very individual. In fact, what is stressful to one person may not be stressful at all to someone else. The following list, however, includes examples of situations that are commonly experienced as stressful:

- Too much to do, such as being expected to complete several tasks in a short period of time.
- Too little to do, such as sitting around all day with no meaningful activities.
- Tense relationships, where people are often arguing or expressing angry feelings or criticizing each other.
- Major life changes, such as losing a loved one, moving away from home, starting a new job, getting married or having a child.
- Financial or legal problems.
- Being sick or fatigued.
- Abusing drugs or alcohol.
- Being the victim or a crime.
- Poverty or poor living conditions.

There is no such thing as a stress-free life, so you can't avoid all stress. In fact, to pursue important goals in your life, it is essential to be willing to take on new challenges, which can be stressful. But it is helpful to be aware of times when you're under stress and to learn strategies for coping with it effectively. The educational handout "Coping with Stress and Common Problems" will go into more detail about this subject.

> *Stress can make symptoms worse or may even trigger the onset of symptoms.*

<u>Question</u>: Have there been times when you were under stress and experienced more symptoms?

What are the goals of treatment?

Because both biological vulnerability and stress contribute to symptoms, treatment for psychiatric symptoms needs to address both of these factors. The main goals of treatment are:

- Reducing biological vulnerability
- Reducing stress
- Coping with stress more effectively

Reducing biological vulnerability

Medications help correct the chemical imbalances which lead to symptoms. There are different medicines to treat different types of symptoms. The educational handout "Using Medication Effectively" provides more specific information about medications and how to get the best results from them.

It is your decision whether to take medication. Medications are not perfect: they don't cure mental illness and they have side effects. Medications also help some people more than others. However, medications are one of the most powerful tools we have for reducing or eliminating symptoms and preventing relapses and rehospitalizations.

Another way to reduce biological vulnerability is to avoid alcohol and drug use. Alcohol and drug use affect neurotransmitters in the brain, which can lead to worse symptoms and relapses. Alcohol and drug use can also lead to legal, financial, and health problems, resulting in stress that can trigger symptoms. In addition, using alcohol and drugs can interfere with the beneficial effects of medication.

> *Medications and avoiding drug and alcohol can reduce biological vulnerability.*

Questions: Have medications helped you to reduce symptoms?
Has avoiding (or decreasing) drug and alcohol use helped you to reduce symptoms?

Reducing stress

Each person experiences stress in his or her own individual way. In addition, what is stressful to one person may not be stressful to another. For example, some people feel stressed by going to a large family gathering, whereas others enjoy it.

In general, the following guidelines are helpful in reducing common sources of stress:

- Identify situations that caused stress for you in the past. Think of ways to handle the situations so they won't be as stressful.
- Set reasonable expectations for yourself—try not to do too much or too little.
- Find activities that are meaningful to you—whether working or volunteering or pursuing hobbies.

- Maintain good health habits by eating well, getting enough sleep, and exercising regularly.
- Seek out supportive relationships where you feel comfortable telling people what you are feeling and thinking.
- Avoid situations where people argue with you or criticize you.
- Give yourself credit for your talents and strengths; don't be hard on yourself.

Reducing stress can help reduce symptoms.

Question: What do you do to reduce stress? You can use the following checklist to answer the question.

Reducing Stress Checklist

Strategy to reduce sources of stress	I use this strategy effectively	I would like to use this strategy or improve the way I use this strategy
Be aware of situations that were stressful in the past		
Set reasonable expectations for myself		
Engage in meaningful activities		
Maintain good health habits		
Seek out supportive relationships		
Avoid situations with arguments and criticism		
Give myself credit for talents and strengths		
Other:		
Other:		

Coping with Stress

Stress is a natural part of life, and everyone experiences it. When stress occurs, however, it is helpful to have some strategies for dealing with it, so it will have a less harmful effect on you. Consider using some of the following strategies for dealing with stress:

- Talk to someone about your feelings.
- Use relaxation techniques, such as deep breathing, meditation, picturing a pleasant scene, progressive muscle relaxation.
- Use "positive self-talk," by saying things to yourself such as "This is a challenge, but I can handle it."
- Keep your sense of humor and try to look at the lighter side. Seek out a funny movie or a book or cartoons.
- Use religion or another form of spiritual inspiration.
- Take a walk or do some other kind of physical exercise.
- Write your thoughts and feelings down in a journal.
- Draw or create other kinds of artwork.
- Think of the situation as a problem to solve, then work on solving the problem.
- Engage in a hobby such as cooking, gardening, reading, or listening to music.

Try to keep an open mind, and experiment with new ways of coping with stress. The more strategies you have, the better you can cope.

Developing strategies for dealing with stress can help reduce symptoms.

Question: What strategies do you use for coping with stress? You can use the following checklist to answer the question.

Coping with Stress Checklist

Strategy for coping with stress	I use this strategy	I would like to try this strategy or improve the way I use it
Talk to someone about my feelings		
Use relaxation techniques		
Use positive self-talk		
Keep a sense of humor		
Use religion or other form of spirituality		
Take a walk or exercise		
Write in a journal		
Express myself artistically		
Work on solving problems		
Engage in a hobby		
Other:		
Other:		

What kinds of treatment options are there to choose from?

There are many reasons for you to be as active as possible in your treatment:

- You are the expert about your own symptoms and what makes you feel better or worse.
- You need to be able to make informed choices about treatment.
- You have a lot to gain by receiving effective treatment.

Depending on your own individual situation and what is available in your community, you can choose among several different treatment options to best serve your needs. Some people choose one or two options; others choose several. A lot depends on your recovery goals.

The following chart lists some of the common recovery goals and the treatment options that may help you move towards achieving your goals. This is only a partial list. The educational handout, "Getting Your Needs Met in the Mental Health System" will cover more options.

Treatment Options

Recovery Goals	Treatment Options to Consider
Finding or maintaining a medication that is effective for me	- Psychiatrist - Medication group - Psychiatric nurse
Getting support and knowledge from other people who have experienced psychiatric symptoms	- Peer support groups - Psychosocial clubhouses - Group therapy - Additional self-help options as listed in the handout "Recovery Strategies"
Getting a job	- Supported employment - Vocational rehabilitation - Volunteer programs - Psychiatric rehabilitation
Solving some personal problems with the help of a professional or group	- Individual therapy - Group therapy
Improving communication skills	- Social skills training groups - Group therapy
Improving family relationships	- Family psychoeducation - Behavioral family therapy
Having structure and activity daily (provided by professionals)	- Partial hospital program

> *The more you learn about treatment,
> the better choices you can make.*

Questions: Which treatment options fit with your recovery goals?
Which of the options are you currently using?
Which would you like to try?

What are some examples of people whose treatment choices work well for them?

Even when people have the same disorder, they may experience symptoms very differently. Therefore, treatment choices vary widely depending on the individual and what works for them. The following are some examples of people whose treatment choices have worked well for them. Your choices may be very different—the important thing is that they work for you.

Example 1:

"I work part-time, and I've noticed that I need to take regular breaks or I start to feel stressed out. I always eat breakfast because if I skip it I start to feel irritable. Exercise helps me relax, so I try to jog every other day, before dinner. Just for 15-20 minutes, but it makes me feel good. I enjoy my life."

"It took a long time to find a medication that worked well for me. But now I take it regularly and it helps me to concentrate better and not feel down all the time. I belong to a support group, which meets twice a month. It helps me to talk to people who have gone through some of the same things I have.

Example 2:

"When I first started to have symptoms and was told the diagnosis, I learned everything I could about it. It helped me to make sense of what was happening, and it also made me feel like I wasn't the only one. I also went to a recovery group that was led by someone who had mental illness. It gave me a lot of hope.

"I've gone to several different doctors, and I think the one I have now is good. She suggested trying one of the newer medicines because it has fewer side effects. I'm considering it. But I don't want to change anything fast.

"I've been seeing a counselor every week to talk about some of the stress I'm under. He taught me how to do some yoga exercises to relax myself after the kids go to bed. I never thought I was the yoga type, but it does make me feel more relaxed."

Example 3

"I go to group therapy every week. A couple of times each week I go to the clubhouse, where I can be with other people and have something fun to do. I've applied for a supported employment program, and I'm really excited about that.

"When I get stressed out, it helps me to sit down with my sketch pad and colored pencils and do some drawing. I put the best drawings up on my wall. I also like to go to the art museums and see paintings and drawings. It takes my mind to a calmer place."

It's important to choose treatment options that work for you as an individual.

Summary of the main points about the stress-vulnerability model and strategies for treatment:

- *Both stress and biology contribute to symptoms.*

- *Biology plays a part in whether someone is vulnerable to developing a mental illness.*

- *Biological factors contribute to the chemical imbalance in the brain that scientists have associated with psychiatric symptoms.*

- *Stress can make symptoms worse or may even trigger the onset of symptoms.*

- *The goals of treatment are to reduce biological vulnerability, reduce stress, and improve the ability to cope with stress.*

- *Medications and avoiding drug and alcohol use can reduce biological vulnerability.*

- *Reducing stress can help reduce symptoms.*

- *Developing coping strategies for dealing with stress can help reduce symptoms.*

- *The more you learn about treatment, the better choices you can make.*

- *It's important to choose treatment options that work for you as an individual.*

Appendix

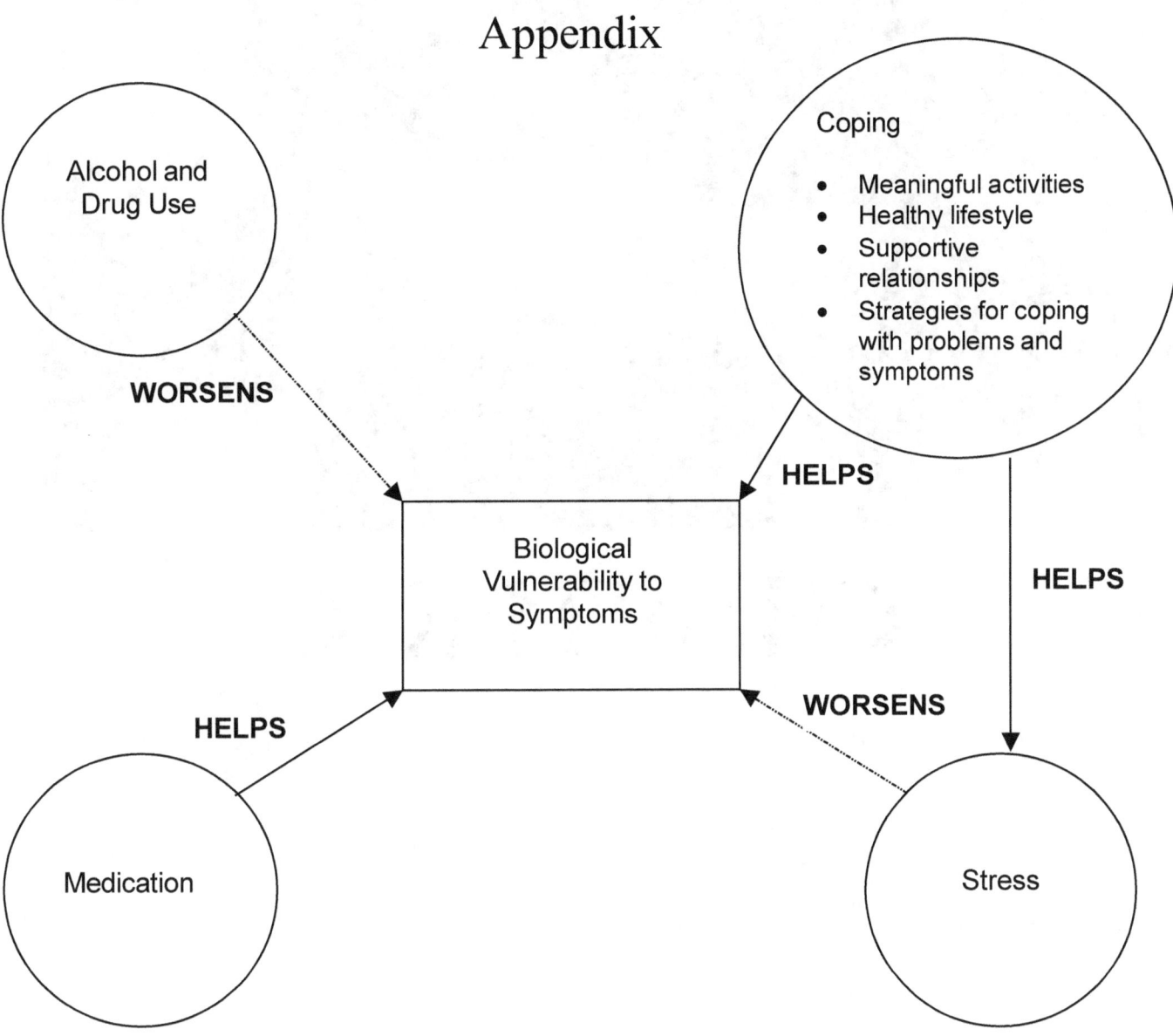

Stress-Vulnerability Model

Building Social Support

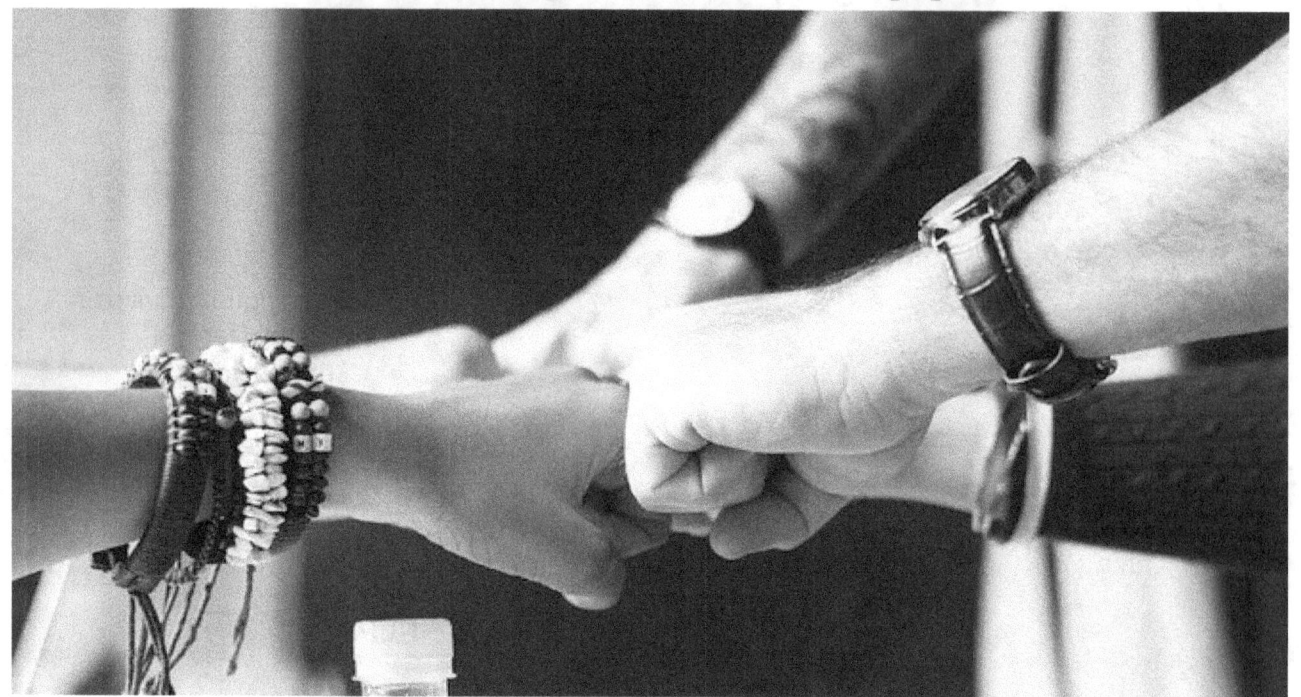

CHAPTER 4

Introduction

This handout discusses how to increase social support in your life. Having social support means that you feel connected and cared for by other people. This is especially important for helping you to reduce stress and reduce relapses. Strategies are described for increasing the number of supportive people in your life and for getting closer to people you already know.

What is social support?

"Social support" refers to having relationships that are rewarding, enriching and helpful. Relationships can be considered "supportive" when they are positively focused and have a minimum of conflict and strife. Differences in opinions are natural in any relationship, and a supportive relationship can involve disagreements from time to time. Disagreements in a supportive relationship, however, can usually be resolved in a peaceful and effective manner.

Social support can come from relationships with a variety of different people, including family members, friends, peers, spouses, boyfriends/girlfriends, co-workers, members of religious or other spiritual groups, classmates, mental health practitioners, and members of peer support groups. Social support systems vary widely.

> *Social support means having relationships that are positive, rewarding and helpful.*

Question: Which of your relationships do you find supportive?

Why is social support important?

Social relationships are an important part of people's lives. For many individuals, the quality of their relationships is a major factor in their personal satisfaction. Supportive relationships make people feel good about themselves and more optimistic about the future. Having supportive relationships can also help people reduce stress. As noted in the handout, "The Stress Vulnerability Model and Strategies for Treatment," reducing stress can help reduce relapses.

> *Relationships are an important part of people's lives.*

> *Supportive relationships can help people reduce stress and reduce relapses.*

Question: How is social support important in your life?

What does social support mean to you?

People have their own individual opinions about what makes a relationship supportive. They also have their own perspectives about what they want from their relationships and whether they are satisfied with the number and quality of their relationships. The following questions may help you evaluate what social support means to you.

Who are the people your life that support you?
What kinds of things do people do that you find supportive?
Which aspects of your relationships are you satisfied with?
Which aspects of your relationships would you like to change?
In what ways are you supportive of other people?
Are you satisfied with the way that you are supportive of other people?
Would you like to have more social support in your life?

Question: Circle the number on the scale below which best describes how satisfied you are with your social support:

/	/	/	/	/
1	2	3	4	5
not satisfied	a little satisfied	satisfied	very satisfied	highly satisfied

Increasing social support

People are often interested in increasing their social support and improving their relationships with others. Two general strategies can be used:

- You can increase the number of people with whom you have contact.

- You can improve the quality of your relationships with people with whom you have regular contact

For many people a combination of both strategies is most helpful.

> Social support can be increased by connecting with more people and improving the quality of existing relationships.

Strategies for connecting with people

Connecting with new people is often the first step towards increasing social support. In order to connect with people, you need to

- Find places to meet people.
- Have interesting things to say.
- Be responsive to what the other person says.

Specific tips for each of these steps are provided below.

Good places to meet people.

You can meet people in all kinds of places. It is helpful to always be on the alert for the possibility of meeting someone, no matter where you are.

While it is possible to meet people in many different places, there are some places to go where meeting people may be easier. These tend to be public places where people naturally gather for recreation, to pursue an interest or to take care of business. Some examples include:

- Community organizations such as libraries or civic associations
- School or class
- Support groups
- Workplace
- Places where people gather for religious or spiritual activities (churches, synagogues, temples, mosques, etc)

- Peer drop-in center
- Health or exercise club such as the YMCA or YWCA
- Parks
- Museums
- Concerts
- Special interest groups such as those relates to politics, hobbies, sports, conservation or recreation
- Bookstores, coffee shops
- Volunteer programs

> *There are many different places to meet new people.*

Questions: Where have you met people before? What places would you like to go to meet new people? You can use the following checklist to record your answers:

Places to Meet People

Places	I have gone to this place to meet people	I would like to go to this place in order to meet people
Community organizations		
School/class		
Support groups		
Church, synagogue, temple, mosque, or other religious place		
Workplace		
Peer drop-in center		
Health or exercise club		
Parks		
Museums		
Concerts		
Special interest groups		
Bookstores, coffee shops		
Volunteer programs		
Other:		

Tips for starting conversations

In order to get to know someone or to get to know someone better, it is helpful to be able to start conversations. Starting and maintaining enjoyable conversations involves a combination of skills. These skills include choosing someone who might be receptive to a conversation, having something interesting to say, and showing interest in the other person.

Some specific tips for conversation are provided below:

- <u>Find someone who isn't occupied</u>.

Choose someone who isn't obviously occupied. If the person is in the middle of doing something, they may not want to stop what they are doing in order to talk to you.

- <u>Choose an interesting topic</u>.

The topic you choose could be related to something that you are doing when you are starting the conversation. For example, if you are in an art gallery, you could start a conversation about the paintings you are looking at.

You could also choose another topic, such as the weather, recent events, or sports. If you don't know the person, you can start by introducing yourself. But as you do so, you should also be thinking of a topic to follow the introduction.

- <u>Look at the person</u>.

Eye contact is important when you are talking to people because it shows them that you are interested in what they have to say. If you feel uncomfortable looking into someone's eyes, you can look somewhere close to their eyes, such as their forehead or nose.

- <u>Smile and nod your head to show you are listening</u>.

It can be helpful to let the person know that you are listening and are interested in what he or she has to say. Showing an interest in the other person indicates that you don't want to dominate the conversation by doing all the talking and that you are receptive to their ideas and point-of-view.

- <u>Tune in to what the other person is saying.</u>

Asking questions about what the other person says and responding to their comments lets them know that you are interested in their perspective. If the person seems uninterested, consider changing topics or politely ending the conversation.

- <u>Avoid telling very personal things about yourself</u>.

When you are just getting to know someone, avoid telling the person very private information about yourself. Such information too early in a conversation sometimes makes the person feel uncomfortable and can make it harder to make a connection with him or her. When you get to know the person better, he or she will feel more comfortable with conversations about more personal topics.

To start a conversation:

- *find someone who isn't occupied*
- *choose an interesting topic*
- *show an interest in what the other person has to say.*

Questions: What strategies do you use when starting conversations?
Which of the conversation strategies would you like to try?
You can use the following checklist to record your answers:

Strategies for Starting Conversations

Strategy	I already do this	I would like to try this or improve the way I do it
Find someone who isn't occupied		
Choose an interesting topic (example:)		
Look at the person		
Smile and nod your head to show you are listening		
Tune in to what the other person is saying		
Avoid telling very personal things about yourself		
Other:		
Other:		

Strategies for getting closer to people

Getting closer to people, including developing friendships and intimate relationships, is an important goal for many people. The most rewarding close relationships are ones in which each person cares about the other person's perspective and well being. In order to be close to other people, it is important to be able to share more personal things about yourself and to be open to them sharing more personal things about themselves with you. It is also important to be willing to do things to help the other person.

Showing the person that you care about him or her is part of being in a close relationship.

Questions: Would you like to develop closer relationships with people?
If so, with whom?

There are three main considerations when you are developing a closer relationship:

- Things you can say to the other person
- Things you can do with the other person (or for the other person)
- Deciding how much and when to disclose personal information about yourself

Things you can say to develop closer relationships

- <u>Express positive feelings and give compliments</u>.

    Telling other people how you feel about them can help bring you closer. This can include expressing and showing affection, but it is not limited to that. For example, you can tell people that you admire certain qualities that they have or that you appreciate specific things about them.

- <u>Ask the person questions about himself or herself</u>.

    Getting to know people and developing closeness involves trying to understand more about their thoughts and feelings. Ask people about what they are thinking and feeling, try to understand their perspective, and show them you are interested in knowing more about them.

- <u>**Tell the person something about yourself**</u>.

    Gradually telling people more things about yourself is part of becoming closer to them. You can tell people about your feelings, your opinions, things you like to do, and your past experiences. Deciding when and what to tell about yourself is discussed below in more detail.

> *To develop closer relationships, it helps to:*
> - *express positive feelings*
> - *ask people questions about themselves*
> - *gradually tell people more about yourself.*

<u>Questions</u>: What are some specific things that you could say to someone to help you get closer to them?
How comfortable do you feel about saying these things?

You can use the following chart to record your answers:

Things You Can Say to Increase Closeness

Types of things you can say	Specific examples of what you could say	How comfortable are you with this?
Expressing positive feelings and giving compliments		
Asking the person questions about themselves		
Telling the person something about yourself		
Other:		
Other:		

Things you can do to develop closer relationships

- Try to understand the other person's point-of-view.

Each person's experience and perspective is unique. To understand someone's point-of-view, it can be helpful to ask yourself questions such as

> "What is the person feeling?"
> "What is the person thinking?"
> "If I were in their shoes, what would I feel or think?"

When you think you understand someone's perspective, it can be helpful to check it out with that person to see if you are correct or not. For example, if someone has been talking about their concerns about starting a new job, you might say something like, "From what you've said, it sounds like you're a little worried about having different responsibilities on the job than you're used to. Is that the way you feel?"

- Do things together.

Identifying activities that you can do together can provide rewarding experiences for both of you. Explore what interests you have in common in order to think of things you can do together.

- **Be willing to compromise.**

In close relationships, neither person can always have their own way. Being willing to compromise and negotiate shows that you are not being selfish and that you care about him or her.

- **Show by your actions that you care about the other person.**

Caring feelings can be expressed by actions as well as words. You can let people know that you care by being helpful, by surprising them in unexpected and pleasant ways, and by investing some of your time in trying to make them happy.

- **Be there for the person and help out.**

"Being there" for someone means being available during a time of need. Everyone has times of need. Recognizing when someone needs help and being able to support and assist him or her is an important sign that you care.

To develop closer relationships with people, it helps to:
- *try to understand their point-of-view*
- *do things together*
- *be willing to compromise*
- *be there for them when they need you.*

<u>Questions</u>: What are some examples of specific things you could do to increase the closeness of your relationships?
How comfortable do you feel about doing these things?

You can use the following chart to record your answers:

Things You Can Do to Increase Closeness

Types of things you can do	Specific examples of what you could do	How comfortable are you with this?
Try to understand the other person's point-of-view		
Do things together		
Be willing to compromise		
Show by your actions that you care about the other person		
Be there for the other person and help out		
Other:		
Other:		

Ways you can disclose personal information to develop closer relationships

"Disclosure" refers to telling someone personal information about yourself. As people get closer to each other, they tell more about themselves. Deciding how much to tell someone can be a tricky decision. If you tell too much too soon, the other person may feel overwhelmed, and may pull away from the relationship. If you disclose too little, over time it may be difficult to have a really close relationship.

In deciding how much to disclose about yourself, it is helpful to keep in mind that when two people are close to each other, they tell each other about the same amount of personal information about themselves. For example, if one person tells about their family background, the other person will usually follow by telling about the same amount about their own family background. You can start by matching the other person's level of disclosure, and then gradually trying to increase the level as you get to know each other better.

It can be helpful to identify three levels of disclosure: low, medium, and high. Low disclosure involves telling things about yourself that are not highly personal, such as your tastes or preferences for things like food, movies, television, or books. High disclosure is telling someone very personal information about yourself, such as having a mental illness. Medium disclosure is somewhere in between.

Deciding what you want to disclose and what you want to keep to yourself is a personal decision based partly on whether you believe the other person will accept you after you have disclosed personal information.

> *Close relationships involve gradually increasing the levels of disclosure between people.*

Questions: Which of your relationships involve low levels of disclosure? Medium levels? High levels? Are there any relationships where you would like to gradually increase the level of disclosure?

You can use the following checklist to record your answers:

Levels of Disclosure in Personal Relationships

Level of disclosure	Relationships you have at this level of disclosure	How satisfied are you with this level of disclosure?
Low level of disclosure		
Medium level of disclosure		
High level of disclosure		

Examples of social support

Example 1:

"I work part-time, and I have enjoyed getting to know some of my co-workers. We talk about work and joke around. Sometimes we give each other rides or take the bus together.

"There's one friend that I've known since high school. He knows what I've been through and we talk about a lot of things, including some of our problems. And we like to do things, like going to the movies.

"I would definitely like to have a girlfriend. I've met a woman that I'm interested in, but so far we're just getting to know each other. I'm trying to take it one step at a time."

Example 2:

"My family is very important to me. That's my mom, my dad, and my two brothers. We've had our ups and downs, like any family, but I feel like they are there for me. If I need to talk, they will listen. If I have a problem, they will help me solve it. I try to do the same for them.

"I've been taking a business class in the evening recently. At first I didn't feel comfortable with the other students, but now that we've been in class together, we have something to talk about. We talk about the assignments where you can pick up coffee on the way to class. Things like that. I look forward to the class now."

Example 3:

"One of my best sources of support right now is other people who have had psychiatric symptoms. I feel like we understand each other very well. They know what I'm talking about and vice versa. I'm a member of a support group and I'm taking a workshop so I can be a leader of a group myself."

> *It's important to develop a support system that works for you as an individual.*

Summary of the main points about building social support

- _Social support means having relationships that are positive, rewarding and helpful._

- _Relationships are an important part of people's lives._

- _Supportive relationships can help people reduce stress and reduce relapses._

- _Social support can be increased by connecting with more people and improving the quality of existing relationships._

- _There are many different places to meet new people._

- _To start a conversation: find someone who isn't occupied, choose an interesting topic, and show an interest in what the other person has to say._

- _Showing the other person that you care about him or her is part of being in a close relationship._

- _To develop closer relationships, it helps to express positive feelings, ask people questions about themselves, and gradually tell them more about yourself._

- _To develop closer relationships with people, it helps to try to understand their point of view, to do things together, to compromise, and to be there for them when they need you._

Using Medication Effectively

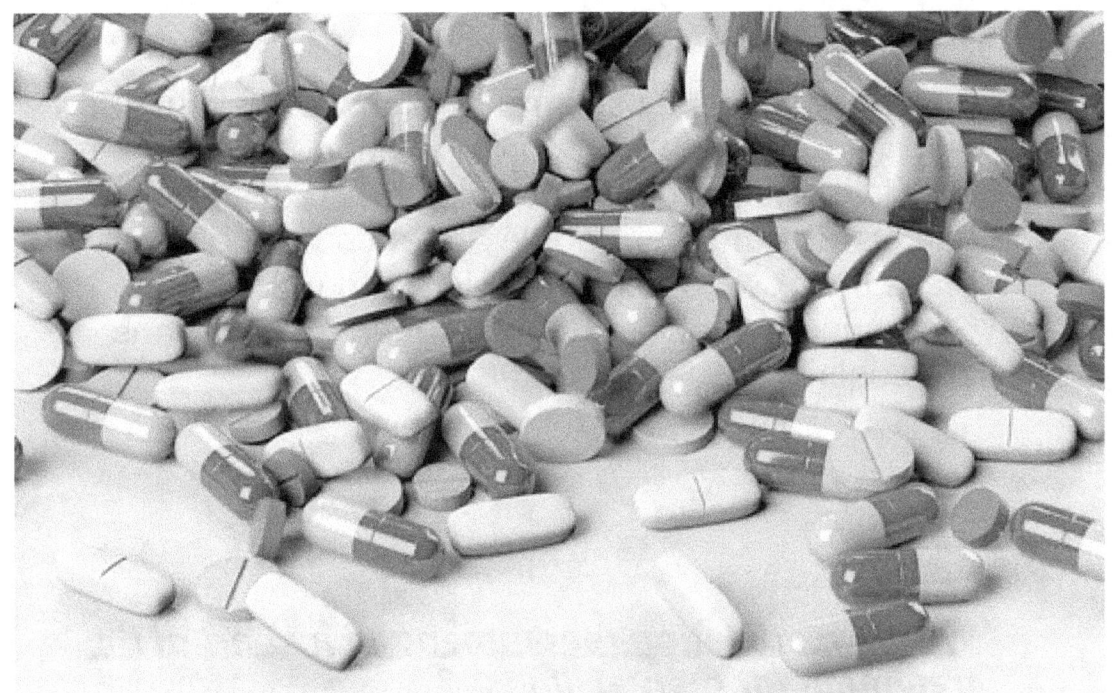

CHAPTER 5

Introduction

This handout discusses medications for psychiatric disorders. Information is provided about the effects of medications, including their advantages and disadvantages. People are encouraged to make their own choices about taking medications. Strategies for getting the most out of medications are described.

Why is medication recommended as part of the treatment for mental illness?

Medications are some of the most powerful tools available for reducing symptoms and decreasing the risk of relapses. When people take medications regularly as part of their treatment, they are less affected by symptoms and they are less likely to have relapses.

In handout #3, you learned about the "stress-vulnerability model." This model is based on evidence that both biological vulnerability and stress contribute to the symptoms of mental illness. Medications reduce biological vulnerability by helping to correct the chemical imbalance in the brain, which leads to symptoms.

When people take medications as part of their treatment, they usually:

- ➢ Experience symptoms less often or less intensely.
- ➢ Concentrate better and think more clearly.
- ➢ Fall asleep more easily and sleep more restfully.
- ➢ Accomplish more of their goals.

> *Medications are some of the most powerful tools available for reducing symptoms and preventing relapses.*

What are your personal beliefs about medication?

People have different beliefs about medication, based on their culture, their family background, and their own experience.

Some people have strong positive beliefs about medications. Make a check mark next to any of following quotations that reflect your beliefs:

_____ *"My uncle is diabetic and takes insulin. He leads a normal life. I have a mental illness and take medication for it. It's the same thing to me."*

_____ *"My medicine helps get rid of the symptoms I was having. It's made a world of difference to my peace of mind."*

_____ *"I tried everything I could on my own— exercise, relaxation techniques, counseling. I was still miserable and depressed until I tried some medicine."*

Other people have strong negative beliefs about medications. Make a check mark next to any of the following quotations, which reflect your beliefs:

_____ *"In my culture, we don't believe in Western medicines. I only want to use herbal remedies."*

_____ *"I'm afraid of the long-term effects on my body of using medications."*

_____ *"It's a matter of will power. I shouldn't need a drug to make me feel better."*

It helps to be aware of your own beliefs about medications, because they can interfere with your being objective. For example, if you have strong positive beliefs about medication, you might not ask enough questions about side effects. If you have strong negative beliefs, you might not find out enough about how the medicine could benefit you.

People may have strong beliefs about medications that can interfere with their making an informed decision.

Question: What do you think about medications?

What are the benefits of medications for mental illness?

Medication has been found to be helpful in two important ways:

- ➢ reducing symptoms during and after an acute episode of the illness
- ➢ reducing the chances of having episodes in the future.

Reducing symptoms during an acute episode

When the symptoms of mental illness are the most severe and troublesome, it is usually described as being a relapse or an acute episode of the illness.
The experience of having relapses varies widely from person to person. Some individuals have only one or a few acute episodes, while others have them more often.

During and after an acute episode, medications can help reduce the severity of the symptoms. Sometimes the medicine helps people quite rapidly, and they are able to relax, think more clearly, and feel less depressed in a few days. Other times it may take a few weeks before the symptoms are reduced significantly.

Reducing the likelihood of relapses

Taking medication on a regular basis helps people prevent relapses of severe symptoms. One person described his medication as a "protective layer between me and the symptoms." Another person said medication "is my insurance policy for staying well."

Taking medication is not a cure for mental illness, and there is no guarantee that you will not have an acute episode again. However, for most people, taking medication on a regular basis significantly reduces their risk of relapses and hospitalizations.

> *Taking psychiatric medications can help to reduce symptoms during an acute episode. When taken on a regular basis, they can reduce the risk of having relapses.*

Question: Have you had an experience where Stopping your medication has been related to worse symptoms or a relapse?

Which medications are used to improve psychiatric symptoms?

Different kinds of medications help different types of symptoms. There are several different types of psychiatric symptoms, and more than one medication may be required to treat them.

There are four major categories of medications, which are commonly used to treat major mental illnesses. The medications and their benefits are summarized on the following chart:

Medications and Their Benefits

Medication Category	Possible benefits
Antidepressants	Can reduce the symptoms of depression, including low mood, poor appetite, sleep problems, low energy and difficulty concentrating. They can also be effective in treating anxiety disorders.
Mood stabilizers	Can help reduce extremes of moods, including mania and depression
Antipsychotic medications	Can reduce the symptoms of psychosis, including hallucinations, delusions, and disorganized speech or behavior.
Antianxiety and sedative medications	Can reduce anxiety, feeling over-stimulated, and difficulty sleeping

At the end of this handout there are appendixes with information sheets containing some types of medications that are available at this time. Please read the information sheets that relate to the medications for the types of symptoms you have experienced. Keep in mind, however, that new medications are being developed all the time. Therefore, it is important to talk to your doctor about what may have become available since the appendix was written.

> *There are four major categories of medications that help improve different types of psychiatric symptoms.*

Questions: Which medications have you taken?
Which symptoms did the medications help you with?
You can use the following checklist to record your answers.

Benefits From Medications I Have Used

Category of medication	Specific medication I used from this category	Benefits I experienced
Antidepressants		
Mood Stabilizers		
Antipsychotics		
Antianxiety or sedatives		
Other category:		

What are the side effects of medication?

It is important to be informed about both the potential benefits and the potential side effects of the specific medication that you have been prescribed. Medications for mental illness, like drugs for treating other illnesses, can cause undesired side effects.

Medication affects people in different ways. Some people may have only a few side effects or no side effects at all from their medication. Others taking the same medication may have significant side effects. Your reaction to medication depends on many factors, including your age, weight, sex, metabolic rate, and other medicines you might be taking.

In most cases, the side effects are temporary, and improve over time as your body adjusts to the medication. Some types of side effects, which are much less common, can be long lasting and even permanent. The newer medications tend to have fewer and less severe side effects. The more serious side effects are associated with the older antipsychotic medications, such as haldol, stelazine and thorazine.

If you recognize that you are having side effects, it is important to contact your doctor as soon as possible. Your doctor needs to help you evaluate how serious the side effects are and what can be done about them.

It is up to you to decide what side effects you can tolerate and what risks you are willing to accept.

When you have side effects, your doctor may advise you to try one of the following: reduce the dose of the medication, add another medication for the side effect, or switch to another medication. There are also some coping strategies for dealing with side effects that help reduce the discomfort or counteract the side effects.

Appendix #5 contains more specific information about side effects and strategies for coping with them.

> *Psychiatric medications can cause side effects.*

Question: What side effects from medications have you experienced?
What did you do when you had side effects?
You can use the following checklist to record your answer.

Side Effects From Medications I have Used

Category of medication	Specific medication I used from this category	Side effects I had when taking this medication
Antidepressants		
Mood stabilizers		
Antipsychotics		
Antianxiety and sedatives		
Other:		

How do you make an informed decision about medication?

You need to make informed decisions about all treatment options, including medication. In making your decision about medications, it is important to learn as much as you can and to weigh the possible benefits and possible drawbacks of taking medication.

Your doctor is vital to your decision-making process. She or he is an expert about medication and has experience helping others find effective medications.

However, it is also important for you to be very active in making decisions about medication. After all, you are the expert about your own experience of mental illness and what makes you feel better or worse.

Therefore, the best method for making a decision involves a partnership between you and your doctor, using both of your expertise's together. It helps to have some questions in mind when you are deciding about taking medication or switching medications. Asking your doctor some of the questions on the following chart may be helpful:

Questions You Can Ask Your Doctor
How will this medication benefit me? What will it help me with?
How long does it take the medication to work? How long before I feel some of the benefits?
What side effects might I get from the medicine? Are there any side effects from long-term use?
What can be done if I get side effects?
Will I need blood tests to make sure that I have the right level of the medication in my bloodstream?
What if the medication doesn't work for me?
Other:

The best way to make a decision about medication is to work in active partnership with your doctor.

Question: What questions would you like to ask your doctor about medications?

From your point of view, what are the pros and cons of taking medication?

To make an informed decision about medications, it is important to weigh the potential benefits (the pros) and the potential drawbacks (the cons) of taking them. The following chart may be useful in summarizing the information:

The Pros and Cons of Taking Medications

Pros of taking medications (the benefits)	Cons of taking medications (the drawbacks)

If you decide to take medications, how can you get the best results?

Many people find that it can be difficult to remember to take medications regularly. "Behavioral tailoring" consists of the following strategies, which are designed to help you to fit taking medications into your regular routine. Since everyone has a different routine, it is important to tailor these strategies to meet your own needs.

> *Simplify your medication schedule as much as possible.*

When you take several medications several times each day, it becomes difficult to keep track of all the doses. Talk to your doctor about making your medication schedule as simple as possible without losing any of the benefits. The fewer the medications you have to take and the fewer the number of times per day, the easier it is to keep track. Some medications are available in long-acting injectible forms that can be administered every two weeks.

Example:

"I used to have a very complicated medication schedule. Four different pills, some twice a day, some three times a day. It was very hard to keep track of. I worked with my doctor to get a medication schedule that was easier for me to manage. Gradually I've gone to taking two different pills, once a day. I hardly ever miss a dose now."

> *Take medications at the same time every day*

Taking the medication at the same time (or times) every day makes it easier to remember. It also keeps the level of medication at a steady level in your bloodstream, which gives you maximum benefit throughout the day.

"I take my pills every night before bed. This helps me to sleep better and to feel better the next day. If I skip a dose, or take it the next morning, I don't feel as well."

> *Build taking medication into your daily routine.*

It is often easier to remember to take medication if it is done in conjunction with another daily activity. Examples of daily activities include brushing your teeth, showering, eating breakfast, and getting ready to go to work.

Example:

"Before I got into a routine, I kept forgetting to take my medicine. Now I make it part of having breakfast before I go to work. I have my cup of coffee, a bowl of cereal, a vitamin and my medication. It's a habit that works for me. I don't have to think about it."

> *Use cues to help yourself remember.*

Many people have developed their own cues to help remind them to take their medications regularly. Some examples of cues include: using a pill container that is organized into daily doses, using a calendar, making notes to yourself, keeping the pill bottle next to an item that is used daily, asking a relative or other supporter to help you remember.

Examples:

"I give myself a cue for remembering to take my medication by putting the bottle next to my toothbrush. Every night when I reach for the toothbrush, I am reminded to take my pills."

"I tape up a note next to the coffee pot, since I take my medication at breakfast.

"My calendar is very important to me. I look at it often to check my schedule for the day. I put a check mark on the date right after I take my medication."

> *Keep the benefits in mind*

Sometimes it helps to remind yourself of the reasons that you have decided to take medications. You could use the checklist "Benefits from Medications I have Used" which is located earlier in this handout.

Example:

"When I start to think that it's a pain in the neck to keep taking medications, I remind myself why I decided to take them in the first place. I don't want to get depressed again, and the medication helps me to do that."

If you decide to take medications, you will get the best results by taking them at the same time every day.

It is helpful to develop strategies for fitting medications into your daily routine.

Questions: If you take medication, what have you found helps you get the best results?
Would it be helpful to try some of the strategies listed above?
You can use the following checklist to record your answer:

Strategies for Getting the Best Results From Medication

Strategy	I have used this strategy	I would like try this strategy or develop it further
Simplify the medication schedule		
Take medications at the same time every day		
Build taking medication into my daily routine		
Use cues and reminders (calendars, notes, pill organizers)		
Remind myself of the benefits of taking medications		
Other:		

Why is medication so complicated?

Everyone responds to medication in different ways. It can take time for you and your doctor to find the medication that helps you the most and has the fewest side effects.

Medications for mental illness usually take time to work. They are not like painkillers, for example, which have an effect within hours. It may take several weeks before you notice a difference in the way you feel. Talk to your doctor on a regular basis about how you are feeling, so that you can work together to find the best medicine for you. At the same time, continue to use as many recovery strategies as possible, such as self help programs, exercising, maintaining a healthy diet, and avoiding stressful environments. See handout #1 for more recovery strategies.

> *It can take time for you and your doctor to find the medication that is most effective for you.*

Examples of individual experiences with medication

Example 1

"I used to go on and off my medication because I didn't think I needed it. I thought, 'Why should I take medicine when I feel fine?' But then I had to go to the hospital for relapses twice in one year. I hated that. Since I've been taking my medicine regularly for the past two years, I haven't had a major relapse and I've been able to stay out of the hospital. I've even begun talking to my doctor about reducing my dose."

Example 2

"I'm still not sure about medication. I only had one episode of symptoms, and I've been feeling pretty much O.K. since then. I check in with my doctor once a week, though, and we're keeping a close eye."

Example 3

"My medicine helps to keep my mood stable. I don't like the side effects, but the doctor and I are working on that. It's just so much better for me not to have those wild mood swings. Now I can have a better relationship with my wife and keep my job. The tradeoff is worth it to me."

Talk to your doctor about any questions or concerns about medications or side effects.

<u>Question:</u> Do you have any questions about medications that you would like to ask your doctor?

Summary of main points about medication:

- *Medications are one of the most powerful tools available for reducing symptoms and preventing relapses.*

- *The best way to make a decision about medication is working in active partnership with your doctor.*

- *People may have strong beliefs about medications that can interfere with their making an informed decision.*

- *Taking psychiatric medications can help to reduce symptoms during and after an acute episode. When taken on a regular basis, they can reduce the risk of having relapses.*

- *There are four major categories of medications, which help improve different types of psychiatric symptoms.*

- *Psychiatric medications can cause side effects.*

- *If you decide to take medications, you will get the best results by taking them at the same time every day.*

- *It is helpful to develop strategies for fitting medications into your daily routine.*

- *It can take time for you and your doctor to find the medication that is most effective for you.*

- *Talk to your doctor about any questions or concerns about medications or side effects.*

Appendix #1: Antipsychotic medications

Antipsychotic medications are sometimes called "major tranquilizers" or "neuroleptics." They are designed to reduce the symptoms of psychosis, including false perceptions (hallucinations), false beliefs (delusions), and confused thinking (thought disorders).

Antipsychotic medications not only help reduce psychotic symptoms during and after an acute episode, but also help prevent relapses and rehospitalizations. They are not addictive. Some of the newer medications also help reduce negative symptoms, including lack of energy, motivation, pleasure, and emotional expressiveness.

Two types of antipsychotic medications are available. The older generation antipsychotics include haldol, moban, mellaril, navane, prolixin, serentil, stelazine, thorazine and trilafon. The newer generation antipsychotics include abilify, clozaril, geodon, risperdal, seroquel, zeldox, and zyprexa. More medications are being developed all the time, so it is important to keep up-to-date with your doctor about what medications are available.

The following chart contains the brand names and chemical names of the antipsychotic medications currently available. Blank spaces are provided to write in the names of new medications as they become available.

Antipsychotic Medications

Brand name	Chemical name
Abilify*	aripiprazole
Clozaril*	clozapine
Geodon*	ziprasidone
Haldol	haloperidol
Loxitane	loxapine
Mellaril	thioridazine
Moban	molindone
Navane	thiothixene
Prolixin	fluphenazine
Risperdal*	risperidone
Serentil	mesoridazine
Seroquel*	quetiapine
Stelazine	trifluoperazine
Thorazine	chlorpromazine
Trilafon	perphenazine
Zyprexa*	olanzapine

* = newer generation antipsychotics

<u>Side effects of antipsychotic medications</u>

People have very different reactions to medications. Some people who take antipsychotic medications experience only a few side effects or none at all. Others experience several. It's also important to keep in mind that each medication has its own side effects, so you need to talk to your doctor about the specific side effects that are associated with the medication that has been recommended to you.

The main advantage of the newer generation medications is that they cause very few of the extrapyramidal (muscle movement) side effects that the older generation medications caused, such as muscle stiffness, mild tremors, restlessness, and muscle spasms. They also cause significantly fewer problems related to sexual difficulties and irregular menstrual periods. However, both the older and newer antipsychotic medications can cause weight gain, and some of the newer ones do so even more. Hypoglycemia and diabetes have recently been found to be possible serious side effects of the newer generation of antipsychotic medications.

Tardive dyskinesia is an undesirable neurological side effect. It causes abnormal muscle movements, primarily in the face, mouth, tongue and hands. Tardive dyskinesia is associated with long-term use of the older antipsychotic medications and ranges from mild to severe. It is important to let your doctor know if you notice any abnormal muscle movements, so that he or she can evaluate for tardive dyskinesia.

Some side effects of antipsychotic medications are rare, but can be very serious if they occur. "Agranulocytosis" is when people stop making the white blood cells needed to fight infections. It is a potentially dangerous side effect of clozaril. However, when regular blood tests are done to monitor white blood cell levels, clozaril can be a very safe medication.

Treatment of Side Effects

When you have side effects, contact your doctor immediately. After discussing the side effects and evaluating how serious they are, he or she may recommend one of the following: reduce the dose of the medication, add a side effect medication, or switch to another medication. The doctor may also suggest some things that you can do to help reduce the discomfort or counteract the side effects. See Appendix #5 for a list of some of these coping strategies.

Web sites for more information about medications

www.mentalhealth.com
www.mentalhealth.about.com
www.drugs.com

Appendix #2: Mood stabilizers

Mood stabilizing medications help treat problems with extremes of moods, including mania and depression. They help to reduce the acute symptoms and also help to prevent relapses and rehospitalizations. They are not addictive.

The following chart lists the most common medications in this category. Blank spaces are provided to fill in the names of any new mood stabilizing medications that become available.

Mood Stabilizing Medications

Brand Name	Chemical Name
Eskalith, Eskalith controlled release	Lithium carbonate
Tegretol	carbamazepine
Depakote, Depakene	valproic acid
Lamictal	lamotrigine

Side effects of mood stabilizers

Not everyone who takes mood stabilizers experiences side effects. However, it is important to be aware of possible side effects and to contact your doctor as soon as you notice them.

Lithium

Possible side effects of lithium include nausea, stomach cramps, thirst, fatigue, headache, and mild tremors. More serious side effects include: vomiting, diarrhea, extreme thirst, muscle twitching, slurred speech, confusion, dizziness, or stupor.

Although lithium is a natural chemical element, like oxygen or iron, it can be harmful if it is taken in too high a dose. To prevent this, the doctor must monitor the amount of lithium in the body by taking regular blood tests.

It is also important to have enough salt in your diet while taking lithium, because the sodium in salt helps to excrete lithium. This means you should avoid low-salt diets and prescription and over-the-counter diuretic medications such as Fluidex with Pamabrom, Aqua-Ban, Tri-Aqua, or Aqua-rid.

Tegretol and Depakote

Possible side effects of Tegretol and Depakote include: fatigue, muscle aching or weakness, dry mouth, constipation or diarrhea, loss of appetite, nausea, skin rash, headache, dizziness, decreased sexual interest, and temporary hair loss.

Some side effects are more serious, including: confusion, fever, jaundice, abnormal bruising or bleeding, swelling of lymph glands, vomiting, and vision problems (such as double vision). It is important to have regular blood tests to monitor the level of these medications, and to check for any changes in blood cells and liver function.

Lamictal

Possible side effects of Lamictal include dizziness, headaches, double vision, unsteadiness nausea, blurred vision, sleepiness, vomiting and a mild rash. These symptoms usually occur when first starting the medication and shortly after an increase in dosage and then often fade. A severe rash should be reported to your doctor immediately.

Because these medications can cause sedation, you must be cautious when driving or operating heavy machinery. It is recommended to limit drinking to one alcoholic drink per week.

Treatment for side effects

When you have side effects, contact your doctor immediately. After discussing the side effects and evaluating how serious they are, he or she may recommend one of the following: reduce the dose of the medication, add a side effect medication, or switch to another medication. The doctor may also suggest some things that you can do to help reduce the discomfort or counteract the side effects. See Appendix #5 for a list of some of these coping strategies.

Web sites for more information about medications
www.mentalhealth.com
www.mentalhealth.about.com
www.drugs.com

Appendix #3: Antidepressants

Antidepressants treat the symptoms of depression, including low mood, low energy, appetite problems, sleep problems, and poor concentration. They help to reduce the acute symptoms and prevent relapses and hospitalizations. Antidepressants can also be effective for the treatment of anxiety disorders such as panic disorder, obsessive compulsive disorder and phobias. They are not addictive.

The newer generation antidepressant medications, such as the family of drugs called serotonin selective reuptake inhibitors (SSRIs) tend to cause fewer side effects. SSRIs include Prozac, Paxil, Zoloft, Serzone, and Luvox. New medications continue to be developed.

The following chart lists the most common antidepressants. Blank spaces are provided to fill in the names of any new antidepressants that become available.

Antidepressant Medications

Brand Name	Chemical Name
Anafranil	clomipramine
Celexa*	citalopram hydrobromide
Cymbalta*	duloxetine
Desyrel	trazodone
Effexor	venlafaxine
Elavil	amitriptyline
Lexapro*	escitalopram oxalate
Ludiomil	maptrotiline
Luvox*	fluvoxamine
Marplan	isocarboxazid
Nardil	phenelzine
Norpramin	desipramine
Pamelor, Aventyl	nortriptyline
Paxil*	paraxitine
Prozac*	fluoxetine
Serzone*	nefazadone
Sinequan, Adapin	doxepin
Tofranil	imipramine
Vivactil	protriptyline
Wellbutrin	buprorion
Zoloft*	sertraline

* = newer generation antidepressants (SSRIs, SSNRIs)

Side effects of antidepressants

Not everyone has side effects when they take antidepressants. But it is important to be aware of them in case you do. Tell your doctor about any of the following side effects: nausea, vomiting, excitement, agitation, headache, sexual problems, dry mouth, dizziness, sedation, weight gain, constipation, heart palpitations, cardiac abnormalities, insomnia, memory problems, overstimulation, hypertensive crisis.

Hypomania, mania and antidepressants

Sometimes a small percentage of people who take antidepressants develop symptoms of hypomania or mania over the course of a few weeks. The symptoms of hypomania include irritability, argumentativeness, agitation, decreased need for sleep, and excessive talking. The symptoms of mania include grandiosity, euphoria, hostility, extreme goal-directed behavior, and engagement in activities that are potentially harmful. If you experience these symptoms, notify your doctor immediately. He or she may lower your dosage of medication or stop it altogether.

Precautions when taking Marplan and Nardil

There are many foods and drugs that should be avoided when taking Marplan and Nardil, including foods that are high in tyramine, such as aged cheeses, aged meats such as salami and pepperoni, and yeast extracts (except when they are baked into breads, etc). You should also avoid drinking beer, Chianti wine, sherry wine and vermouth and taking certain medications such as Tegretol, Dopar, Sinemet, Demerol, Aldomet, Ritalin, decongestants and stimulants. It is important to obtain a complete list from your doctor of drugs and foods to avoid.

Although it is unusual, occasionally people develop carpal tunnel syndrome when they take Marplan or Nardil. This can be corrected by appropriate vitamin supplements.

Treatment of side effects

When you have side effects, contact your doctor immediately. After discussing the side effects and evaluating how serious they are, he or she may recommend one of the following: reduce the dose of the medication, add a side effect medication, or switch to another medication. The doctor may also suggest some things that you can do to help reduce the discomfort or counteract the side effects. See Appendix #5 for a list of some of these coping strategies.

For more information about medications

www.mentalhealth.com
www.mentalhealth.about.com

Appendix #4: Antianxiety and sedative Medications

Antianxiety and sedative medications help reduce anxiety and feeling overly stimulated. Some of these medications also help people sleep.

Unlike other medications for mental illnesses, these medications take only one to two hours to take effect. Also unlike other medications for mental illnesses, some antianxiety and sedative medications can be addictive and long-termuse should generally be avoided. If these medications are used, they should be carefully monitored.

The following chart lists the most common medications used for antianxiety and sedation. Blank spaces are provided to fill in the names of any new medications that become available. It is important to note that some of the medications can be used to help both anxiety and sleep problems, while others are used to help only one of these problems. Also, some of these medications are addictive, while others are not. It is important to talk to your doctor about the specific benefits and side effects of the medication you are taking.

Antianxiety and Sedative Medications

Brand Name	Chemical Name
Ativan	lorazepam
Benadryl	diphenhydramine
Buspar	buspirone
Centrax	prazepam
Dalmane	flurazepam
Halcion	triazolam
Klonopin	clonazepam
Librium	chlordiazepoxide
Noctec	Chloral hydrate
Restoril	temazepam
Serax	oxazepam
Valium	diazepam
Xanax	alprazolam

Side effects of antianxiety and sedative medications

Not everyone has side effects when they take antianxiety or sedative medications. It's important to be aware of them if you do, however, and to talk to your doctor right away. The most common side effects are over-sedation, fatigue, and problems with memory or other cognitive abilities. Because of the sedating effect, you are advised to limit drinking no more than one alcoholic drink per week. You are also advised to be cautious when driving. As mentioned earlier, long-term use of some of these medications can lead to dependency.

Treatment of side effects

When you have side effects, contact your doctor immediately. After discussing the side effects and evaluating how serious they are, he or she may recommend one of the following: reduce the dose of the medication, add a side effect medication, or switch to another medication. The doctor may also suggest some things that you can do to help reduce the discomfort or counteract the side effects. See Appendix #5 for a list of some of these coping strategies.

Web sites for more information about medications

www.mentalhealth.com
www.mentalhealth.about.com
www.drugs.com

Appendix #5: Coping with Side effects

The following charts list some of the common side effects of different categories of medications and some suggestions for coping with them or counteracting them. Blank spaces are provided for additional strategies that you find useful.

Coping with Side Effects of Psychiatric Medications

Side effect	Strategy
Drowsiness	Schedule a brief nap during the day. Get some mild, outdoor exercise, such as walking. Ask your doctor about taking medication in the evening
Increased appetite and weight gain	Emphasize healthy foods in your diet, such as fruits, vegetables and grains. Cut down on sodas, desserts and fast foods. Engage in regular exercise. Go on a diet with a friend or join a weight reduction program.
Extreme restlessness	Find a vigorous activity that you enjoy, such as jogging, skating, aerobics, sports, outdoor gardening, swimming, bicycling
Muscle stiffness	Try doing regular muscle stretching exercises or yoga or isometrics exercises
Dizziness	Avoid getting up quickly from a sitting or lying down position.

Blurry vision	For mild blurry vision, talk to your doctor about getting reading glasses. These can often be bought without a prescription at a local drug store for very little money.
Sensitivity to the sun	Stay in the shade, use sunscreen and wear protective clothing. Avoid going out at the sunniest time of day.
Shakiness or tremors	Avoid filling cups and glasses to the brim.
Dry mouth	Chew sugarless gum, suck on sugarless hard candy, or take frequent sips of water.
Constipation	Drink 6-8 glasses of water daily. Eat high fiber foods such as bran cereals, whole grain breads, fruits and vegetables. Do light exercise daily.
Other:	
Other:	
Other:	

Drug and Alcohol Use

CHAPTER 6

Introduction

Using alcohol, such as drinking a beer, a glass of wine, or a mixed drink, is common in modern society. Similarly, using certain types of street drugs is also common, such as marijuana, cocaine, amphetamines ("speed"), and hallucinogens (such as LSD and "ecstasy"). Although using these types of substances can make people feel good, they can also cause problems and make it more difficult for people to manage their psychiatric illness. This module focuses on the effects of drug and alcohol use on mental illness and other parts of life, and offers strategies for reducing these effects.

Commonly Used Substances and Their Effects

It is helpful to understand what people commonly experience when they use alcohol and drugs. The following table lists both the positive and negative effects of alcohol and drugs.

COMMONLY USED SUBSTANCES AND THEIR EFFECTS

Substance Type	Examples	Positive Effects	Negative Effects
Alcohol	Beer, wine, gin, whiskey, vodka, tequila	-Relaxation -Lighter mood	-Slower reaction time, drowsiness -Socially embarrassing behavior
Cannabis	Marijuana, hash, THC	-Relaxation -"High" feeling	-Slower reaction time and poor coordination -Apathy and fatigue -Paranoia -Anxiety or panic feelings
Stimulants	Cocaine (powder or crack), amphetamines (crystal meth., Dexedrine)	-Alert feeling -Euphoria, good feelings	-Anxiety -Paranoia and psychosis -Sleeplessness
Hallucinogens	LSD, ecstasy, peyote, mescaline	-Heightened sensory awareness -Feeling of well-being	-Bad "trips" -Psychotic symptoms
Opiates	Heroin, opium, morphine, Vicodin, Demerol, Oxycontin	-Feeling of well-being -Relaxation -Reduced pain sensitivity	-Drowsiness -Highly addictive -Risk of overdose

OTHER COMMONLY USED SUBSTANCES AND THEIR EFFECTS

Substance Type	Examples	Positive Effects	Negative Effects
Inhalants	Glue, aerosols, paint	-"High" feeling	-Severe disorientation -Toxic/brain damage
Caffeine	Coffee, some teas, some sodas	-Alert feeling	-Feeling jittery -Can interfere with sleep
Nicotine	Smoking, chewing tobacco	-Feeling alert -Feels good	-Causes many health problems
Benzodiazepines (Anti-anxiety medication)	Valium, Xanax, Klonopin Ativan	-Reduced anxiety -Relaxation	-Rebound anxiety when medication wears off -Loss of inhibition and coordination -Dulled senses

Why do People Use Alcohol and Drugs?

People have used mind-altering substances such as alcohol for thousands of years, since the beginning of civilization. People use alcohol and drugs for a number of different reasons.

➢ To socialize

Sometimes people use substances in social situations, just for fun. Alcohol and other substances are also sometimes used to celebrate holidays (like New Years Eve or the Fourth of July) or a special occasion (such as a birthday, anniversary, or job promotion). Some people drink or use drugs to be accepted by others, to have friends and to avoid loneliness.

➢ To improve their mood

Another reason some people use alcohol or drugs is simply that they make them feel good, at least temporarily. Some substances make people feel more alert and energetic. Other substances make people feel tranquil and satisfied, or alter one's perceptions of the world around them.

➢ To cope with symptoms

Yet another reason people use alcohol and drugs is to cope with negative feelings or troubling symptoms. Substances may be used to deal with feelings of depression or anxiety. Or people may use substances to escape from hearing voices or other hallucinations. For some people, using substances may help them get to sleep when they have trouble sleeping. Other people may use substances because it helps them focus their attention.

> ➢ To distract themselves from problems

People may also use substances as a way of distracting themselves from problem situations or unpleasant parts of their lives. For example, some people use alcohol or drugs to distract themselves when they are having conflict with others, when they are under high levels of stress, when they are dissatisfied with parts of their lives (such as not working, not having a nice place to live, or not having good friends), or when they are unhappy with themselves. For these individuals, substance use provides a temporary escape from life problems.

> ➢ It becomes part of their daily routine

One more reason some people use substances is that it becomes part of their daily routine, and gives them something to look forward to. Everybody needs to have things they care about and look forward to doing, and for some people this includes using alcohol or drugs. For these individuals, using alcohol or drugs is more than just a habit; it is part of their lifestyle and an important part of how they live each day. Some people, have too much free time and they slip into using drugs and alcohol as a way to pass the time.

> PEOPLE USE SUBSTANCES FOR MANY DIFFERENT REASONS:
> - TO SOCIALIZE
> - TO CELEBRATE
> - BECAUSE IT FEELS GOOD
> - TO COPE WITH BAD FEELINGS OR SYMPTOMS
> - TO DISTRACT THEMSELVES FROM PROBLEM SITUATIONS
> - TO HAVE SOMETHING TO DO

People use substances for a number of different reasons. You can use Checklist 1 to list the substances you use and to check off the reasons that you use them.

Checklist 1

Reasons for Using Alcohol or Drugs

Reason for Using:	Substance #1: _____	Substance #2: _____	Substance #3: _____
Feeling less depressed			
Feeling "high"			
Feeling more alert			
Feeling good			
Reducing pain			
Reducing anxiety			
Coping with hallucinations			
Altering my senses			
Sleeping better			
Distracting myself from problems			
Coping with symptoms			
Feeling sociable			
Something to do with friends			
Something to do every day			
Celebrating			
Avoiding boredom			
Peer pressure			
Other:			

Substance Use and the Stress-Vulnerability Model

Using alcohol and drugs is common. However, these substances can interfere with the ability of people to manage their mental illness. The stress-vulnerability model of mental illness explains how using substances can make the symptoms of mental illness worse.

The symptoms of mental illness are caused by biological factors (or vulnerabilities). These biological factors can be made <u>worse</u> by:
- alcohol and drugs
- stress

These biological factors can be made better by:
- medications
- effective coping
- social support
- meaningful activities

Alcohol and drug use can make symptoms worse and cause relapses. Using these substances can also interfere with medications, making them less effective at reducing symptoms and preventing relapses. Because even small amounts of alcohol or drug use can cause these problems, people with psychiatric illness may be putting themselves at a significant risk of setting off symptoms when they use.

SOME PEOPLE WITH MENTAL ILLNESS ARE SUPER SENSITIVE TO THE EFFECTS OF ALCOHOL AND DRUGS

What are some problems related to alcohol and drug use?

The positive effects of using substances are well known, such as the way they can make people feel good and provide a temporary escape from unhappiness. However, using substances can also have negative effects and can interfere with having a good quality of life. Understanding both the positive and negative effects of using substances can help in deciding whether to change this habit. Some of the common problems related to drug and alcohol use are described below.

> Increased symptoms/relapses

Using substances can *bring on symptoms*, or *make symptoms worse*. Common symptoms that can be worsened from using substances include depression, anxiety, hallucinations, delusions, and thinking difficulties. Sometimes increases in symptoms can lead to relapses and re-hospitalizations.

> Social problems

Substance use can cause *conflicts with other people*. People may have disagreements about someone's use of substances, or be worried that the person uses too much. Substance use can also make people less predictable and harder to get along with. For example, someone may be very irritable because he has a craving to use substances. Or someone may be late coming home because she was using substances.
Using substances can result in other social problems as well. Sometimes people are not able to meet others' expectations because they are using substances, such as being a good parent, keeping the house clean, or preparing family meals. Using substances can also

cause problems related to hanging out with the wrong types of people. For example, using substances with others may increase the chances of being arrested due to their illegal behavior, being evicted from housing, or being taken advantage of either sexually or financially. People may act like they are your friends, but only because you have something they want, such as your money or the use of your apartment.

➤ <u>Interference with work or school</u>

Using drugs and alcohol sometimes *gets in the way of work or going to school*. People may have difficulty focusing at work and doing their job well. Or they may be late or have absences from work due to using substances the night before. Using substances can also make it hard to focus on schoolwork and can contribute to dropping out of school.

➤ <u>Daily living problems</u>

Sometimes when people use substances they have a harder time *taking care of themselves*. They may not shower, brush their teeth, or keep up their appearance like they ordinarily would. People sometimes do not eat well when they're using substances. They may also not take care of their living space, such as their room or their apartment.

> Legal problems

Using substances can cause *legal problems*. Driving under the influence of alcohol or drugs is against the law and can result in severe penalties. People can also be arrested for possessing illegal drugs. Drug and alcohol use can cause other legal problems. Sometimes parents with substance use problems have their children taken away from them, or may face restrictions on their ability to see or parent their children. Using disability money, such as SSI or SSDI, on drugs or alcohol can lead to restrictions on access to that money, and the need to have a representative payee (or some other legal representative) manage one's money.

> Health problems

Using substances can lead to a variety of *health problems.* Long-term alcohol use can produce many problems, including liver problems such as cirrhosis. The use of some substances such as cocaine, heroin, and amphetamines is linked to infectious diseases such as hepatitis C and the HIV virus. These are blood-borne diseases that can be spread through exposure to an infected person's blood, such as by sharing needles (injecting) or straws (snorting) for using these drugs. When people have substance use problems, they often neglect to take care of chronic health conditions such as diabetes and heart disease. Because of the physical effects of using substances and the neglect of one's health, substance use can shorten one's lifespan.

➢ Safety problems

Sometimes people use substances in situations that are not safe. For example, driving under the influence of alcohol or drugs can be dangerous. Similarly, operating heavy machinery when under the influence of substances can be dangerous. Finally, people sometimes put themselves in risky situations in order to obtain substances, such as going to bad neighborhoods, and associating with people who may take advantage of them or harm them.

➢ Psychological dependence

Using alcohol or drugs can play an important part in people's lives. *Psychological dependence* refers to when someone spends a great deal of time using substances, gives up important activities in order to use, often uses more than intended, or has repeatedly tried to stop unsuccessfully in the past.

➢ Physical dependence

When people use substances often, they may need to take larger amounts to get the same effect, because they develop a *tolerance* to the substance. They may also experience withdrawal symptoms if they don't use the substance, such as feeling shaky or nauseous.
These are symptoms of *physical dependence*.

USING SUBSTANCES CAN CAUSE:
- Symptom relapses and rehospitalizations
- Social problems
- Work/School difficulties
- Daily living problems
- Poor self-care
- Health problems
- Legal problems
- Safety problems
- Psychological or physical dependence

Using substances can interfere with having a good quality of life. You can use Checklist 2 to list the substances you commonly use and to check off the negative effects that you have had from using these substances.

Checklist 2

Negative Results from Using Alcohol and Drugs

Negative results from drug or alcohol use:	Substance #1: _____	Substance #2: _____	Substance #3: _____
Relapses			
Hospitalization			
My symptoms get worse			
I have conflicts with others			
People complain about my use			
I get more irritated at others			
People can't count on me			
I lose friends			
I hang out with a bad crowd			
People take advantage of me			
I don't take good care of myself			
I spend too much money			
I have legal problems			
I have health problems			
I lost housing			
I do unsafe things			
I had problems with my job			
Alcohol and drugs take over my life			
My relationships suffered			
Other:			

Weighing the Pros and Cons of Using Substances

Deciding to stop using alcohol and drugs can be a difficult decision to make. There are some positive aspects to using substances, such as socializing and feeling good, but negative aspects as well. One way to help you make a decision about using alcohol and drugs is to come up with a list of all the "pros" (advantages) of using substances, and all the "cons" (disadvantages) of using substances. To best understand your own pros and cons for <u>using substances</u>, complete Worksheet 1 on the following page. You can use the information on Checklist 1 and Checklist 2 to help list the pros and cons on the worksheet.

WORKSHEET 1

Pros and Cons of Using Substances

"PROS" of using substances List all the advantages of continuing to use drugs and alcohol. (Consider advantages such as: socializing, feeling good, escaping, coping with symptoms, something to look forward to, habit, and any others that might be important.)	"CONS" of using substances List all the disadvantages you can think of for using substances. (Consider disadvantages such as: worse symptoms or relapse of mental illness, conflict with family or friends, trouble with work or school, parenting difficulties, problems with health, legal system, housing, or money.)

Considering all the pros and cons of using substances, would you like to cut down/stop?

_____ NO. I do not want to cut down or stop.

_____ MAYBE. I think I might want to cut down or stop but I'm not sure.

_____ YES. I would like to cut down or stop.

Deciding Whether to Cut Down or Stop Using Substances

Understanding the pros and cons of using substances can help you decide whether you want to continue using. It is also helpful to consider the pros and cons of <u>not</u> using substances. What are the advantages of developing a sober lifestyle? What would you have to give up in order to develop such a sober lifestyle? On the following page, complete Worksheet 2 to consider the pros and cons of <u>becoming sober.</u>

WORKSHEET 2

Pros and Cons of Sobriety

PROS of becoming sober List all the advantages to developing a sober lifestyle. Consider how sobriety may help you achieve personal recovery goals, such as better control of your mental illness, better relationships, more independence, better health, ability to work and go to school, better parenting, fewer legal, housing, money, or health problems.	CONS of becoming sober List what you think you might have to give up if you stop using substances. Consider the "costs" of sobriety, such as losing friends, nothing fun to do, troubling symptoms, no escape, and feeling bad.

Considering all the pros and cons of sobriety you listed above and the pros and cons of using substances (Worksheet 1), would you like to cut down/stop?

_____ NO. I do not want to cut down or stop.

_____ MAYBE. I think I might want to cut down or stop but I'm not sure.

____ YES. I would like to stop.

Developing a Sober Lifestyle

When people decide to develop a sober lifestyle, it takes planning and practice. Sometimes there can be setbacks along the way, such as urges to use substances or relapses in substance use. Developing your own personal plan for a sober lifestyle is an important part of managing your mental illness and achieving your personal recovery goals. There are three important steps to achieving sobriety:

➢ Remember your reasons for not using substances.
➢ Develop a plan to prevent going back to using substances in "high risk" situations.
➢ Identify new ways of getting your needs met.

Tips for accomplishing each of these steps are provided below:

Identifying Personal Reasons For Not Using Substances

Whenever someone decides to cut down or stop using substances, it is important for them to identify their personal reasons for wanting a sober lifestyle, and to regularly remind themselves of these reasons. In what ways could sobriety help you achieve your personal recovery goals? Consider possible reasons such as:
- Better ability to manage mental illness (fewer relapses)
- Improved social relationships
- Improved ability to work or go to school
- Having your own apartment
- Being a better parent
- Fewer legal problems
- More money to spend on other things

Dealing With "High Risk" Situations

In order to be successful in stopping substance use, it is helpful to make plans about how to deal with situations in which one has used substances in the past. These situations, sometimes called *"high risk situations,"* often involve other people, but not always.

- Being offered substances by friends
- Being pressured to use substances by friends or acquaintances
- Running into a former drug connection
- Holidays
- Going to a party
- Having money in your pocket
- Feeling bad (such as feeling depressed, anxious or frustrated)
- Having nothing to do
- Spending too much time alone
- Remembering good times related to substance use

Avoiding these situations can reduce the risk of relapse. However, complete avoidance is not always possible. Effective strategies for dealing with "high risk" situations are critical to developing a successful sobriety plan. Specific high-risk situations are described below, along with some possible strategies to manage those situations.

- ➢ Social situations involving offers or pressures to use substances:
    - Decline in a firm voice tone
    - Don't make excuses for "no" (it invites debate)
    - Repeat the refusal if needed
    - Offer an alternative activity if it is a friend
    - Level with friends/relatives about the importance of your sobriety and ask them to respect it
    - Leave the situation if necessary

- ➢ Having cravings to use substances:
    - Distract yourself by doing something that focuses your attention elsewhere
    - Cheerlead with self-talk, "I can cope," etc.
    - Use relaxation techniques until cravings pass
    - Use prayer
    - Contact a friend

- ➢ Having money in your pocket:
    - Plan ways to keep most of your money in a safe place and at a distance from you
    - Problem-solve ways to avoid direct access to money

- ➢ When things aren't going well, such as experiencing depression, anxiety, hallucinations or sleep problems:
    - Depression
        - *Schedule pleasant activities
        - *Challenge negative thinking
        - *Exercise
        - *Use positive self-statements
    - Anxiety
        - *Use relaxation techniques
        - *Challenge thoughts that cause you to worry
        - *Gradually expose yourself to feared but safe situations

- Hallucinations
    - *Distract yourself with other activities
    - *Accept the voices or other hallucinations without giving them undue attention or control over your life
    - *Use relaxation to tolerate the distress
- Sleep problems
    - *Avoid caffeine use in the afternoon
    - *Avoid naps
    - *Go to bed at the same time each night
    - *Develop a pleasant nighttime routine (e.g. reading, watching TV)

Finding New Ways of Getting Your Needs Met

In order to develop a sober lifestyle, it is important to develop new ways of getting your needs met that do not involve using substances. Common reasons for using substances include:
- Socializing with others
- Feeling accepted by other people
- Feeling good
- Escaping boredom
- Dealing with bad feelings
- Help with sleeping
- Having something to do and look forward to

Developing new ways of getting your needs met is hard work. The Illness Management and Recovery program is aimed at helping you develop new strategies for meeting your needs, including social needs, coping with symptoms, and doing other interesting things with your time. Developing new ways of getting your needs met can take time and effort. However, the rewards of a sober lifestyle and the ability to achieve personal recovery goals make the effort worthwhile.

Examples of People Who Are Achieving Personal Recovery Goals

When people begin to adopt a sober lifestyle it can be encouraging to hear about others who have made this decision and experienced some of the benefits. Reading the following examples may be helpful.

"I used to think alcohol was my best friend, but now I know better. It was always there when I needed it, and I organized my life around drinking, either alone or with other people. But drinking cost me a lot—it made my symptoms worse and caused hospitalizations. I couldn't hold down a job, and I couldn't take care of my kids. Now that I'm sober I'm back in control of my life. I've stayed out of the hospital, I'm working again, and I can be a better mother, and role model, for my kids."

Glorissa, 38 years old with bipolar disorder, sober for 8 years.

"Getting off drugs was tough going for me. I thought using drugs was the solution to all my problems, either getting high or zoning out. Learning new ways of dealing with my depression, my voices, and my sleep problems helped me control my urges to use drugs. I had to make new friends, too, and these friends seem to really care about me. I feel a lot better about myself now that I have my own apartment and I'm going back to school."

Jerome, 28 with schizoaffective disorder, sober from cocaine (crack), speed, and marijuana for 14 months.

Question: Whom do you know who has made positive changes by developing a sober lifestyle?

Abstinence or Cutting Down?

Deciding to take control over one's life by addressing problems related to drug or alcohol use is an important decision that involves changing one's lifestyle. Part of making such a decision involves deciding whether to stop using substances altogether (abstinence) or to cut down but not stop using entirely.

People with substance use problems often find it difficult to cut down on using substances, because using even a small amount makes them want to have more. In addition, because of the biological nature of psychiatric disorders, people with a mental illness can be very <u>sensitive</u> to the effects of even small amounts of alcohol and drugs. This means that those small amounts of substances can have drastic effects. For this reason, many people with drug and alcohol problems are more successful developing an abstinent lifestyle rather than cutting down how much they use.

Some people want to work on their substance use problems, but are not ready to stop using completely. For these people, reducing the amount of alcohol or drugs that they use can be a good first step towards sobriety.

ABSTINENCE IS THE BEST WAY OF

OVERCOMING

SUBSTANCE USE PROBLEMS

Question: Have you (or someone you know) tried to cut down or stop using substances in the past?
What happened?

Making a Personal Sobriety Plan

In order to achieve your sobriety goals, it is helpful to develop a specific plan. This plan should include the three steps described above: identifying your reasons for wanting to stop using substances, coming up with strategies for dealing with situations in which you have previously used substances, and developing other ways of getting your needs met that do not involve using substances. Worksheet 3, on the following page, can be used to help you develop your personal sobriety plan.

WORKSHEET 3

Personal Sobriety Plan

CONGRATULATIONS! You've taken the first and most important step toward ridding your life of problems related to alcohol and drugs. Complete this plan by following the steps outlined below. You can change or modify your plan based on how well it is working for you. Share your plan with people who are close to you so they can support you in achieving your goals of sobriety.

Step 1. List one to three reasons how your life will be better by stopping using substances. Consider how sobriety may help you achieve your personal recovery goals.

_____
_____
_____

Step 2. Identify one to three "high risk" situations that can lead to unwanted use of alcohol or drugs. Consider situations in which you have used substances in the past, such as people offering you substances, being pressured to use, feeling bad, having nothing to do, and cravings.

_____
_____
_____

Step 3. Make a plan for how to deal with those "high risk" substance use situations. For each "high risk" situation, identify one or two ways of dealing with it.

Situation 1:

_____
_____

Plan for dealing with it:

_____
_____
_____
_____

Situation 2:

_____
_____

Plan for dealing with it:

_____
_____
_____
_____

Situation 3:

_____
_____

Plan for dealing with it:

_____
_____
_____

Step 4. Find new ways of getting your needs met. Consider the ways substances have met your needs in the past, such as hanging out with friends, feeling relaxed or "high," dealing with symptoms, or having something to do. What needs did they meet? For each need you identify, think of at least one new strategy for getting that need met.

Need 1:

_____
_____

Strategy for meeting this need:

_____
_____
_____

Need 2:

_____
_____

Strategy for meeting this need:

_____
_____
_____

Need 3.

_____
_____

Strategy for meeting this need:

_____
_____
_____

Recovery from Substance Use Problems

Taking control over your life and tackling your substance use problems can be hard work, and there may be setbacks along the way. However, your strength and determination will pay off as you become sober and reclaim your life. You have every right to be hopeful that recovery is possible, and that you can take charge of your own life and grow past the effects that substances have had on it!

Reducing Relapses

CHAPTER 7

Introduction

This handout discusses strategies for reducing symptom relapses or minimizing the severity of any relapses that occur. In order to reduce relapses it is helpful to identify stressful situations that have contributed to relapses in the past. It is also helpful to identify your own personal warning signs of an impending relapse. This information can be combined to develop a relapse prevention plan. This plan can be even more effective by including a significant other, such as a relative or friend.

Why do people have relapses?

The symptoms of mental illness tend to vary in intensity over time. Sometimes the symptoms may be absent; sometimes they may be mild or moderate; sometimes they may be strong.

When psychiatric symptoms become severe, it is usually referred to as a "relapse" or an "acute episode of the illness." Some relapses can be managed at home, but other relapses require hospitalization to protect the person or other people.

Mental illness affects people in very different ways. Some people have a milder form of their illness and only have an episode once or a few times in their lives. Other people have stronger forms of their illness and have several episodes, some of which require hospitalization. Some people constantly experience symptoms, but do not have severe episodes that require hospitalization.

Scientists have not been able to identify all the reasons that people have relapses of their symptoms. Research has shown, however, that relapses are more likely to occur when:

- People are under more stress
- People stop taking their medications
- People use alcohol or drugs

> *Mental illnesses tend to be episodic, with symptoms varying in intensity over time.*

Preventing and reducing relapses

There are many things you can do to prevent or reduce relapses. You have already learned some important relapse reduction strategies in the earlier educational handouts, including the following:

- Learn as much as possible about your illness.
- Be aware of your own individual symptoms.
- Be conscious of when you are under stress and develop strategies for coping with stress.
- Participate in treatments that help you recover.
- Build social supports.
- Use medication effectively.

In this handout you will learn some additional helpful strategies for staying well:

- Recognize events or situations that contributed to relapses in the past.
- Recognize the early warning signs that you might be starting to have a relapse.
- Develop your own relapse prevention plan to respond to early warning signs.
- Use the help of other people, such as family members, professionals, and friends, to prevent early warning signs from becoming full-blown relapses.

> *Different strategies can be used to prevent or reduce relapses.*

What are common events or situations that can "trigger" relapses?

Some people can identify certain events or situations that appear to have led to relapses in the past. The events or situations that seemed to contribute to relapses can be thought of as "triggering" relapses.

The following chart lists some examples of common triggers. Please check off the examples that reflect an experience you have had.

Examples of Common Triggers

Personal Descriptions of Triggers	I experienced something like this
"I noticed that when I started staying out late, and not getting enough rest, I tended to relapse."	
"When I'm under more stress at work, like having strict deadlines, I'm likely to start having symptoms again."	
"Every time I go back to drinking beers every night, I end up needing to go back to the hospital."	
"When there's a change in my life, even a good change like moving into a better apartment, I tend to feel stressed out. Then the symptoms seem to come back."	
"If I have arguments with my boyfriend, it really brings me down. Sometimes the symptoms get worse then."	
"The biggest problem for me is when I stop taking medicine. I decide that I'm feeling better and there's no need to take medicine any more. Before long, the symptoms start again."	
Other:	
Other:	

Once you have identified a situation that appeared to trigger a relapse in the past, it is helpful to think about how you might handle the situation differently if it were to occur again. For example, if you noticed that drinking beers with your friends tends to trigger an episode, you could plan some activities with them that do not involve drinking. If you noticed that being under stress tends to trigger an episode, you could plan to use a specific relaxation technique, such as deep breathing, the next time you encounter another stressful situation.

> *Identifying situations and events that triggered relapses in the past can help you reduce the risk of future relapses.*

Questions: Have you experienced any relapses of symptoms?
Are you able to identify situations or events that triggered relapses in the past?
If so, what could you do to handle the situation differently?

What are "early warning signs"?

Even when people do their best to avoid it, their symptoms may start to come back and they may have a relapse. Some relapses may occur over short periods of time, such as a few days, with very little or no warning. However, most relapses develop gradually over longer periods of time, such as over several weeks.

There are often changes in the person's inner experience and changes in their behavior when a relapse is starting. For some people, the changes may be so subtle at first that they may not seem worth noticing. For others, the changes are more pronounced and distressing. When people look back after a relapse, they often realize that these early changes, even the subtle ones, were signs that they were starting to have a relapse. These changes are called "early warning signs."

Early warning signs are the subtle changes in a person's inner experience and behavior that signal that a relapse may be starting.

Question: Have you experienced any relapses of your symptoms?
If you have, did you notice any early signs of your relapses?

What are some common early warning signs?

Some early warning signs are quite common. Others are more unusual. The following chart lists some examples of the more common early warning signs. Please check off the examples that reflect an experience you have had.

Examples of Common Early Warning Signs

Early warning sign	Individual Example	I experienced something like this
Feeling tense or nervous	"Even going to the playground with my kids made me nervous. It seemed like the merry-go-round was going faster and that there were accidents waiting to happen everywhere."	
Eating less or eating more	"First I started skipping breakfast. Then I started skipping lunch. I lost weight even though I wasn't trying."	
Decreased need for sleep	"When I started to relapse, I didn't feel like I needed sleep. I would start working on my inventions and stay up all night."	
Trouble sleeping too much or too little	"I was tired and wanted badly to sleep. But somehow I couldn't fall asleep. I was exhausted all the time."	
Feeling depressed or low	"I started to feel that my work wasn't any good. And that I wasn't a good person. I couldn't take pleasure in anything. My mood was sliding down and down."	
Social withdrawal	"I only wanted to be alone. I even waited to eat dinner until my roommates had gone to bed."	
Feeling irritable	"Even the smallest things would irritate me. For instance, I would fly off the handle if my husband called to say he was going to be 15 minutes late. I had no patience."	

Stopping medication	"I stopped taking my medicine. I even threw away the bottles. I stopped going to my support group."	
Trouble concentrating	"Knitting usually relaxes me. But I couldn't concentrate enough to do the stitches right. My mind was wandering."	
Thinking that people are against you	"It seemed like people behind the counter at the fast food restaurant were talking about me. They even seemed to be laughing at me. I couldn't understand why."	
Hearing voices	"The voice was not loud at first. Sometimes it just said my name."	
Drug or alcohol use or abuse	"Usually I don't drink. But when I was starting to relapse, I found myself pouring a drink of scotch every night. I think I was just trying to get in a better mood."	
Increased spending or shopping	"I used up my checking account and then charged two credit cards to their limits."	
Being overconfident about your abilities	"I thought I was such a great driver that the traffic laws didn't apply to me. I was stopped by the police going 30 miles over the speed limit."	
Other:		
Other:		

Common early warning signs include:

- *Feeling tense or nervous*
- *Eating less or eating more*
- *Trouble sleeping too much or too little*
- *Decreased need for sleep*
- *Feeling depressed or low*
- *Feeling like not being around people*
- *Feeling irritable*
- *Stopping treatment*
- *Trouble concentrating*
- *Thinking that people are against you*
- *Drug or alcohol use or abuse*
- *Increased spending or shopping*
- *Being overconfident about your abilities*

<u>Question:</u> Have you experienced any of the common early warning signs? Which ones?

What are some other early warning signs?

Some people have early warning signs that others don't have. These unique warning signs are equally important to recognize.

Some examples of unique warning signs are:

"Before my last two episodes, I cut my hair very, very short."

"My brother noticed that I was whistling all the time."

"I started buying lottery tickets two or three times a day."

"I started wearing the same clothes every day. The same khaki pants and blue T-shirt."

"I became preoccupied with martial arts. I practiced martial arts moves for hours."

> *Some people have early warning signs that are unique.*

Questions: Have you experienced early warning signs that other people don't have? If so, what are your unique early warning signs?

Is there a systematic way to identify your own warning signs?

The following checklist contains a list of common early warning signs. Check off the early warning signs that you experienced in the week before your last relapse.

Early Signs Questionnaire
(Adapted with permission, Herz and Melville, 2001)

Early warning signs	I experienced this sign
My mood shifted back and forth.	
My energy level was high.	
My energy level was low.	
I lost interest in doing things.	
I lost interest in the way I looked or dressed.	
I felt discouraged about the future.	
I had trouble concentrating or thinking straight.	
My thoughts were so fast I couldn't keep up with them.	
I was afraid I was going crazy.	
I was puzzled or confused about what was going on around me.	
I felt distant from my family and friends.	
I had the feeling that I didn't fit in.	
Religion became more meaningful to me than before.	
I felt afraid that something bad was about to happen.	
I felt that other people had difficulty understanding what I was saying.	
I felt lonely.	
I was bothered by thoughts I couldn't get rid of.	

I felt overwhelmed by demands or felt that too much was being asked of me.	
I felt bored.	
I had trouble sleeping.	
I felt bad for no reason.	
I was worried that I had physical problems.	
I felt tense and nervous.	
I got angry at little things.	
I had trouble sitting still. I had to keep moving or pace up and down.	
I felt depressed and worthless.	
I had trouble remembering things.	
I was eating less than usual.	
I heard voices or saw things that others didn't hear or see.	
I thought that people were staring at me or talking about me.	
I had a decreased need for sleep.	
I was more irritable.	
I was overconfident about my abilities.	
I increased my spending or shopping.	
Other:	
Other:	

Do people always recognize that they are experiencing early warning signs?

People are not always aware when their behavior has changed and they are experiencing an early warning sign of relapse. For example, someone might not realize that he or she is feeling unusually irritable. Instead, it may seem to him or her that other people are being especially annoying.

Friends, family members, co-workers, healthcare practitioners and other supportive people often notice when someone seems different or is acting out of character. They can be helpful allies in recognizing early warning signs.

If you ask them, your family members, friends and mental health practitioners can be your "extra eyes and ears" for noticing early warning signs. You can tell them some possible early warning signs to look for, and let them know that you would like them to inform you when they notice these signs. You can also include them in your "relapse prevention plan" to help you take action to keep early warning signs from becoming relapses.

> *Family members, friends, mental health practitioners and other supporters can help you recognize early warning signs.*

Question: Whom would you like to help you recognize early warning signs? You can use the following chart to record your answer.

People Who Could Help Me Recognize Early Warning Signs

Friends?
Family members?
Support group members?
Practitioners?
Co-workers?
Spouse or significant other?
Others?

What can be done when you become aware that you are experiencing an early warning sign of relapse?

The more quickly you act on early warning signs, the more likely it is that you can avoid a full relapse.

When early warning signs are noted, it helps to ask yourself the following questions:

- Is my stress level high? What can I do to reduce it?
- Am I taking part in the treatments I chose? Am I going to my support group, doing my relaxation exercises, going to my appointments with my counselor, etc.?
- If medication is part of my treatment, am I taking my medication as prescribed? If not, how can I make sure I do?
- Should I arrange a special appointment to talk to the doctor? Do I need to start a medication? Do I need a higher dose of the medication I am taking?
- Should I contact someone for extra support?

The following list contains examples of what other people have done when they recognized they were experiencing early warning signs. Some examples may sound familiar to you.

- "When I started to feel so irritable with everyone, even my best friend, I realized that I was under a lot of stress with changes at the office. I talked with my practitioner about strategies for coping with the stress better so it didn't affect me so much."

- "First someone called from my synagogue, asking why I hadn't been coming to services like I used to. Then someone from my support group called and asked why I hadn't been coming for the past three weeks. I realized that something might be wrong. I decided to go to the next support group, and asked a friend to give me a ride."

- "I thought my medicine wasn't helping me. So I didn't renew the prescription when it ran out. My thinking got very confused. I kept forgetting things, too. I called the pharmacist about getting the medicine renewed, and then I called the doctor to talk about what had happened."

- "My brother noticed empty beer bottles in the kitchen when he came to visit. When we got to talking, I realized that I was starting to use alcohol to help me fall asleep. The next day I called my counselor."

The more quickly you act on early warning signs, the more likely you can avoid a full relapse.

Question: Have you had an experience where you were able to avoid early warning signs from becoming full relapses?
If so, what did you do?

How can you make a Relapse Prevention Plan?

It's not possible to predict who will have only one or two acute episodes of the symptoms of mental illness and who will have more. Making a Relapse Prevention Plan can help you avoid relapses and minimize the severity of episodes that do occur.

In developing a Relapse Prevention Plan, you may find it helpful to consult with the supportive people in your life. Peers, practitioners, family members, and others can help you remember details about what helped in past situations and can make suggestions about possible steps to take if early warning signs appear.

Support persons can also have a part in the plan itself, if you want them to. For example, you might ask family members to let you know if they notice early warning signs or ask them to help you reduce stress by taking walk with you. Of course, you make the final decision about what you want in your plan and whom you want involved.

Plans for preventing relapses are most effective if they contain the following:

- *Reminders of past triggers*
- *Reminders of past early warning signs*
- *What helps you when you're having an early warning sign*
- *Who you would like to assist you*
- *Who you would like contacted in an emergency*

The following pages contain an example of a Relapse Prevention Plan completed by Alberto.

Relapse Prevention Plan: Alberto's Example
Reminder of events or situations that triggered episodes in the past: • broke up with my girlfriend • smoked marijuana
Reminder of early warning signs that I experienced in the past: • felt tense, irritable • thought people were picking on me, didn't like me • couldn't concentrate on TV
What I think would help me if I am experiencing an early warning sign: • If I'm smoking marijuana again, I need to stop, and maybe go back to my "Double Trouble" group. • If I'm upset about something that happened, I need to talk to my friend Juan or to my brother Martin. • If I'm feeling stressed out, I need to make sure I'm doing something to relax me every day, like listening to music or biking. • If I start to feel like people are picking on me or I can't concentrate, I need to talk to my counselor. • If I still don't feel better, I need to consider more medication—at least for a short time.
Who I would like to help me, and what I would like them to do: • Juan or Martin could tell me if they think I'm starting to get irritable. • Juan could go biking with me. • My counselor could help me think of ways to relax. • My doctor could help me decide if I need more medicine.
Who I would like to be contacted in case of an emergency: • Martin, my brother, ###-#### • Maria Rodriguez, my counselor, ###-#### • Dr. Rose, my doctor, ###-####

Before developing his Relapse Prevention Plan, Alberto talked with the supportive people in his life (his friend, his brother, his counselor, and his doctor). He asked them what they had observed before his last relapse and included some of their observations in his list of early warning signs. He also asked for their suggestions in making a plan for responding to an early warning sign and asked them whether they would be willing to play a specific part in carrying out the plan.

After writing up his Relapse Prevention Plan, Alberto asked his friend, his brother, his counselor and his doctor to read it. He then gave copies to each of them. Alberto keeps a copy of his Relapse Prevention Plan in his desk drawer, where he also keeps his checkbook. Whenever he writes a check, he makes a point of looking over his plan.

A Relapse Prevention Plan can help you in case early warning signs appear. The plan should contain:

- *Reminders of past triggers*
- *Reminders of past early warning signs*
- *What helps you when you're having an early warning sign*
- *Who you would like to assist you*
- *Who you would like contacted in an emergency*

> *It can be very helpful to have friends, family members, practitioners and other supporters involved in making the Relapse Prevention Plan and helping to carry it out.*

Questions: What would you include in your Relapse Prevention Plan?
You can use the following planning sheet to record your answer.

Relapse Prevention Plan
Reminder of events or situations that triggered relapses in the past: 1. 2. 3. 4.
Reminder of early warning signs that I experienced in the past: 1. 2. 3. 4
What I think would help me if I am experiencing an early warning sign: 1. 2. 3. 4.
Who I would like to assist me, and what I would like them to do: 1. 2. 3. 4.
Who would I like to be contacted in case of an emergency? 1. 2. 3. 4.

Examples of people who have been able to prevent or reduce the number of relapses they experience

David

"My strongest early warning signs are having vivid, bizarre dreams and not being able to sleep. When that happens, I start doing things to keep myself calm, like taking walks and listening to music. I give my checkbook and credit card to my parents because then I won't be able to go on spending sprees and buy things I don't need. Doing artwork helps, but I try not to work on projects late at night, because that makes it harder to go to sleep. If I need to, I call my doctor. Sometimes having some extra medication has helped me avoid a relapse. These things might not work for everyone, but they have kept me well."

Tamika

"I've noticed that I start to feel down about myself. I can't think of anything good about the present, and I keep dwelling on the past. I don't understand why, but I start thinking about a boy I dated in high school, even though that was over 15 years ago. I've found that it helps to talk to someone, like my sister, about what I'm feeling, instead of keeping it to myself. It also helps me to schedule something every day that gets me out of the house. Even if it's just going to the post office to mail a letter, it's better than staying inside those four walls at home. Going to support groups helps, because they understand what I'm feeling. If it gets to the point I'm thinking about life not being worth living, I know it's gotten very serious. I call my doctor right away. For over two years I've been able to avoid a relapse."

A Relapse Prevention Plan can help you avoid having relapses of your symptoms.

<u>Question</u>: What do you think will help you most in reducing the risk of relapse?

Summary of main points about preventing or reducing relapses

- *Mental illnesses tend to be episodic, with symptoms varying in intensity over time.*

- *Different strategies can be used to prevent or reduce relapses.*

- *Identifying situations and events that triggered relapses in the past can help you reduce the risk of future relapses.*

- *Early warning signs are the subtle changes in a person's inner experience and behavior that signal that a relapse may be starting.*

- *Common early warning signs include:*

    - *Feeling tense or nervous*
    - *Eating less or eating more*
    - *Trouble sleeping or sleeping too much*
    - *Decreased need for sleep*
    - *Feeling depressed or low*
    - *Feeling like not being around people*
    - *Feeling irritable*
    - *Stopping treatment*
    - *Trouble concentrating*
    - *Thinking that people are against you*
    - *Drug or alcohol use or abuse*
    - *Increased spending or shopping*
    - *Being overconfident about your abilities*

- *Some people have early warning signs that are unique.*

- *Family members, friends, mental health practitioners and other supporters can help you recognize early warning signs of relapse.*

- *The more quickly you act on early warning signs, the more likely you can avoid a full relapse*

- *A Relapse Prevention Plan can help you in case early warning signs appear. The plan should contain:*

    - *Reminders of past triggers*
    - *Reminders of past early warning signs*
    - *What helps you when you're having an early warning sign*
    - *Who you would like to assist you*
    - *Who you would like contacted in an emergency*

- *Friends, family members, practitioners and other supportive people can be helpful in developing your Relapse Prevention Plan and carrying it out.*

- *A Relapse Prevention Plan can help you avoid having relapses of your symptoms.*

Coping with Stress

CHAPTER 8

Introduction

This handout describes different ways of coping effectively with stress. In order to cope effectively, it is first important to know what situations you find stressful and what the experience of stress is like for you. Specific strategies for dealing with stress are suggested, such as using relaxation techniques, talking with others, exercising, and creative expression.

What is stress?

"Stress" is a term people often use to describe a feeling of pressure, strain, or tension. People often say that they are "under stress" or feel "stressed out" when they are dealing with challenging situations or events.

Everyone encounters stressful situations. Sometimes the stress comes from something positive (like a new job, new apartment, or new relationship) and sometimes from something negative (like being bored, having an argument with someone, or being the victim of crime).

> *Stress is the feeling of pressure, strain or tension that comes from dealing with challenging situations.*

Question: What is it like when you experience stress?

Why is stress relevant to mental illness?

According to the stress-vulnerability model, stress is an important factor in mental illness because it can worsen symptoms and lead to relapses. If you can decrease stress, you can decrease symptoms.

Nobody has a stress-free life and probably nobody would want to! Stress is a natural part of life. In fact, to pursue important personal goals, you need to be willing to take on new challenges, which can be stressful. Being able to cope effectively with stressful situations can minimize the effects of stress on you and your symptoms. This can enable you to continue to pursue your goals and enjoy life.

> *Coping effectively with stress can help you to reduce symptoms and pursue your goals.*

What makes you feel under stress?

Different people find different things stressful. For example, some people enjoy the hustle and bustle of a big city, while others don't like the crowds and noise and find it stressful. Some people enjoy going to a party and meeting new people; others find it stressful. Knowing what you personally find stressful will help you cope better.

There are two main types of stress: life events and daily hassles.

Life events refers to experiences such as moving, getting married, the death of a loved one, or having a baby. Some life events are more stressful than others; for example, getting a divorce is usually more stressful than changing jobs.

To see how many life events you have experienced in the past year, complete the following checklist:

Life Events Checklist

Put a check mark next to each event that you have experienced in the past year.

____ Moving
____ Getting married
____ New baby
____ Divorce or separation
____ Injury
____ Illness
____ New job
____ Loss of a job
____ Inheriting or winning money
____ Financial problems
____ Injury or illness of a loved one
____ Death of a loved one
____ Victim of a crime
____ Legal problems
____ New boyfriend or girlfriend
____ Broke up with a boyfriend or girlfriend
____ Stopped smoking
____ Went on a diet
____ New responsibilities at home
____ New responsibilities at work
____ No place to live
____ Hospitalization
____ Drinking or using street drugs caused problems
____ other:_____

____ Total number of life events checked off.

moderate stress=1 event

high stress=2-3 events

very high stress=more than 3 events

<u>Daily hassles</u> are the small daily stresses of everyday life that can add up if they occur over time. Examples of daily hassles include dealing with long bus rides, working with unpleasant or critical people, having conflicts with family members or close friends, living or working in a noisy chaotic place, and being rushed to do things.

The following checklist will help you evaluate how many daily hassles you are dealing with:

Daily Hassles Checklist

Place a check mark next to each event that you have experienced in the past week:

- ____ not enough money to take care of necessities
- ____ not enough money to spend on leisure
- ____ crowded living situation
- ____ crowded public transportation
- ____ long drives or traffic back ups
- ____ feeling rushed at home
- ____ feeling rushed at work
- ____ arguments at home
- ____ arguments at work
- ____ doing business with unpleasant people (sales clerks, waiters/waitresses, transit clerks, toll booth collectors)
- ____ noisy situation at home
- ____ noisy situation at work
- ____ not enough privacy at home
- ____ minor medical problems
- ____ lack of order or cleanliness at home
- ____ lack of order or cleanliness at work
- ____ unpleasant chores at home
- ____ unpleasant chores at work
- ____ living in a dangerous neighborhood
- ____ other:_____

____ Total number of hassles in the past week

moderate stress=1 or 2 daily hassles

high stress=3-6 daily hassles

very high stress=more than 6

> *Life events and daily hassles are both sources of stress.*

Questions: What is the most stressful life event you have experienced in the past year?

What are the most stressful daily hassles you have experienced in the past week?

What are the signs that you're under stress?

When people are under stress, it affects them physically and emotionally. It also affects their thinking, mood, and behavior. Some people show only physical signs of stress, such as muscular tension, headaches or sleep problems. Others have trouble concentrating or become irritable, anxious or depressed. Still others may pace or bite their nails. Each person's response to stress is individual.

Being aware of your own personal signs of stress can be very helpful, because once you realize that you're under stress you can start to do something about it.

You can use the following checklist to identify your own personal signs of being under stress.

Signs of Stress Checklist

Put a check mark next to the signs you notice when you are under stress:

- ____ headaches
- ____ sweating
- ____ increased heart rate
- ____ back pain
- ____ change in appetite
- ____ difficulty falling asleep
- ____ increased need for sleep
- ____ trembling or shaking
- ____ digestion problems
- ____ stomach aches
- ____ dry mouth
- ____ problems concentrating
- ____ anger over relatively minor things
- ____ irritable
- ____ anxious
- ____ feeling restless or "keyed up"
- ____ tearful
- ____ forgetful
- ____ prone to accidents
- ____ using alcohol or drugs (or wanting to)
- ____ other:_____
- ____ other:_____
- ____ other:_____

> *Being aware of signs of stress can help you take steps to prevent it from getting worse.*

Question: Have you noticed any signs of being under stress in the past week?

How can you prevent stress?

Putting energy into preventing stress can pay off. If you eliminate some of the avoidable stress in your life, it frees you up to enjoy yourself more and to accomplish more of your goals.

Most people find it helpful to be familiar with a variety of prevention strategies, like the ones described below and listed in the "Strategies for Preventing Stress Checklist." Choose the strategies that best suit you.

<u>Be aware of situations that caused stress in the past</u>. If you found a situation stressful before, it will probably cause problems again. Knowing that a situation has been stressful will allow you to think of different ways to handle it so it won't be as stressful. For example, if you notice that you become irritable whenever you catch the bus at rush hour, try catching it at a less busy time. Or try practicing deep breathing if you become tense on a crowded bus.

If large holiday gatherings with your extended family make you feel tense, try taking short breaks away from the larger group. Or try getting together with family members at times other than holidays, in smaller groups.

<u>Schedule meaningful, enjoyable activities.</u> Having activities that you enjoy makes a significant difference in reducing stress. For some people, their work is meaningful and enjoyable. Other people look to volunteering, hobbies, music, sports

or art for meaning and enjoyment. It all depends on what the individual finds most meaningful.

Schedule time for relaxation. It's important to take time to relax each day, to refresh your mind and body from the tensions of the day. Some people find exercise relaxing, while others find reading or doing a puzzle or some other activity to be relaxing.

Have balance in your daily life. Being active and involved is important to keeping stress low. However, too much activity can lead to stress. It's important to leave time for sleep and for restful, relaxing activities, such as a reading or taking a walk.

Develop a support system. Seek out people who are encouraging and supportive, rather than critical and pressuring. It's very helpful to have relationships with people you feel comfortable with. Common support systems include, friends, family members, peer support, professionals and members of one's religious or spiritual group. See the handout "Building Social Supports" for more information on this subject.

Take care of your health. Eating well, getting enough sleep, exercising regularly, and avoiding alcohol or drug abuse helps prevent stress. These healthy habits are not easy to maintain, but they really pay off.

Talk about your feelings or write them down in a journal. Holding in your feelings can be very stressful. It helps to have an outlet for your feelings so that you don't keep them bottled up. These may be positive feelings, like being excited about a new job or negative feelings, such as being angry at how someone else has behaved. Having someone to talk to, such as a family member, friend, or professional, can help. Or you might find it helpful to keep a journal of your thoughts and feelings.

<u>Avoid being hard on yourself</u>. Some people increase their stress by being critical of themselves and what they are accomplishing. Try to be reasonable about what you expect from yourself, and give yourself credit for your talents and strengths. It can be helpful to identify some positive features about yourself and remind yourself of these features when you are feeling negatively about yourself.

Strategies for Preventing Stress Checklist

Strategy	I already use this strategy	I would like to try this strategy or develop it further
Be aware of situations that caused stress in the past		
Schedule meaningful activities		
Schedule time for relaxation		
Have a balance in my daily life		
Develop my support system		
Take care of my health		
Talk about my feelings		
Write down my feelings in a journal		
Avoid being hard on myself. Identify positive features about myself		
Other:		

> *You can avoid stress by using strategies such as scheduling enjoyable activities and developing a support system.*

Question: Which prevention strategies would be most helpful to you?

How can you cope with stress effectively?

Coping effectively with stress is a key to living a successful and rewarding life and being able to pursue your personal goals. Some examples of strategies for coping with stress include:

Talking to someone about the stress you are experiencing

"When I was packing up my stuff to move to a new place, I started having headaches and trouble sleeping. I called my sister and told her how stressed out I felt. She told me she felt the same way when she moved the last time. She even offered to help me pack. It made a huge difference."

Using relaxation techniques

"If I've had a stressful day, it helps me to do some deep breathing. I put on some relaxing music, and sit in my favorite chair. Then I start by taking ten deep, slow breaths. Then I let my breath out very slowly. As I exhale, I try to imagine that when I let out my breath, I'm letting out the tension in my body. Then I take about 20 or 30 more breaths. Sometimes I try to imagine a peaceful scene, like the ocean, when I'm breathing. I usually feel more relaxed after that."

The Appendix to this handout contains some relaxation techniques that you can try.

Using positive self-talk

"Before when I was under stress, I used to blame myself and think that there was no way out. Now I try to think more positively. I say to myself, 'This is hard, but I can do it,' or 'If I take this one step at a time, I'll be able to handle it.' It's hard to do sometimes, but it makes me feel better about myself."

Maintaining your sense of humor

"For me 'laughter is the best medicine.' When I've been on a subway ride that lasted two hours instead of 45 minutes, I feel very tense and agitated. I have some funny videos at home, and I'll pull one out and have a good laugh. Believe it or not, it helps me to watch a Monty Python movie or one starring Adam Sandler."

Participating in religion or spiritual activity

"I grew up in a religious home. Although I'm not sure I believe every aspect of that religion, I still find it comforting to go to services. And sometimes instead of going to services I go for a walk in the park and see how beautiful nature can be. That's very spiritual for me."

Exercising

"I like to 'work off' my stress by getting some exercise. Sometimes I go for a run and sometimes I just do some jumping jacks until I calm down."

Writing in a journal

"I've started keeping a journal to write down my thoughts and feelings. I don't care about the grammar or spelling—I just write down what comes into my head. Sometimes I write about stressful things and that seems to help. Writing helps me think things through."

Making or listening to music

"I'm a music person. I put on my headphones and blow away the stress of the day. I can even do it on the train, to distract myself on the long ride."

Doing art or going to see art

"I like to sketch. I especially like drawing cartoons. I must admit I sometimes make some unflattering cartoons of people who are bugging me."

Playing games or developing a hobby

"I like playing card games. When I don't have anyone to play with, I like solitaire. It's relaxing to me."

Using coping strategies, such as listening to music, exercising, watching videos, or participating in a hobby, can help you manage stress effectively and enjoy your life.

Questions: What strategies do you use to cope with stress?
What strategies would you like to try or develop further?
You can use the following checklist to record your answer to these questions.

Strategies for Coping with Stress Checklist

Strategy	I already use this strategy	I would like to try this strategy or develop it further
Talking to someone		
Using relaxation techniques		
Using positive self talk		
Maintaining my sense of humor		
Participating in religion or other form of spirituality		
Exercising		
Writing in a journal		
Listening to music		
Doing artwork or going to see artwork		
Participating in a hobby		
Other:		
Other:		

Examples of coping effectively with stress

People develop different strategies for coping with stress, depending on what works for them. The following individuals have recognized what kinds of situations are stressful to them and have worked out strategies that help them cope effectively with these situations.

Leticia

"For me, it's very stressful to rush to get somewhere on time. I start to feel anxious and irritable. Sometimes I even get a headache. So I try to plan ahead as much as possible, and allow myself plenty of time. On the nights before I go to work, I lay out my clothing for the next day. I get up at least an hour before I have to leave the house to catch the bus. Then I don't feel anxious. I can relax on my way to work and start the day feeling fresh.

"Of course, I can't plan for everything. Sometimes the bus is late or the road conditions are bad. When I feel myself starting to get anxious, I do some deep breathing to slow myself down. Sometimes I use 'positive self-talk.' I tell myself, 'I have an excellent record at work of arriving on time and doing my job well. It's O.K. if I'm late once in a while. My boss has always told not to worry about this. Just relax.' It works for me."

Daniel

"Recently I've been under stress because my mother has been ill and in the hospital. I visit her almost every afternoon and I think I'm doing all I can to help her. But sometimes I have trouble sleeping. I lie in bed worrying, so it takes me longer to fall asleep. Then I end up tired in the morning and have a hard time getting up.

"It helps me to talk to someone about my worries. I talk to my sister and it helps a lot. I also try to do something relaxing in the evening, to take my mind off Mom's illness. If it's not too dark, I take a walk in the neighborhood. Or I might read a travel magazine or watch a nature show on TV. It helps me to feel more calm and to be able to fall asleep more easily."

Ching-Li

"I feel tense when there is a lot of noise. I try to avoid those kinds of situations. But there are times when it's unavoidable, like at my apartment. I have roommates, and sometimes they watch television shows or make noise when they are cooking dinner. I like my roommates and I don't think they are being excessive. Noise is just part of having roommates.

"It helps me to take a break and go to my room. I like to listen to my music on headphones; it drowns out the noise and takes me to a more quiet place."

You can develop an individual plan for coping with stress that works for you.

How to develop a plan for coping with stress

This handout included checklists to help you identify the following: stressful situations, signs of stress, strategies for preventing stress, and strategies for coping with stress. It may be helpful to put this information together as an individual plan for coping with stress using the following form:

Individual Plan for Coping with Stress

Stressful situations to be aware of:
1.

2.

3.

Signs that I am under stress:
1.

2.

3.

My strategies for <u>preventing</u> stress:
1.

2.

3.

My strategies for <u>coping</u> with stress:
1.

2.

3.

Summary of the main points about coping with stress

- *Stress is the feeling of pressure, strain, or tension that comes from responding to challenging situations.*

- *Being able to cope effectively with stress can help you to reduce symptoms and pursue your goals.*

- *Life events and daily hassles are both sources of stress.*

- *Being aware of signs of stress can help you take steps to prevent it from getting worse.*

- *You can avoid stress by using strategies such as scheduling enjoyable activities and developing a support system.*

- *Using coping strategies, such as listening to music, exercising, watching videos, or participating in a hobby, can help you manage stress effectively and enjoy your life.*

- *You can develop an individual plan for coping with stress that works for you.*

Appendix: Relaxation Techniques

Three types of relaxation techniques are described below:

- Relaxed breathing
- Muscle relaxation
- Imagining a peaceful scene

Relaxation techniques are most effective when they are practiced on a regular basis. When you are first learning a technique, you usually concentrate on doing the steps according to the instructions. As you become familiar with the instructions, you will be able to concentrate more on the relaxation you are experiencing. Choose one of the following techniques and try practicing it daily. After a week, evaluate whether you think the technique is effective for you.

Relaxed Breathing

The goal of this exercise is to slow down your breathing, especially your exhaling.

Steps:

- Choose a word that you associate with relaxation, such as CALM or RELAX or PEACEFUL.

- Inhale through your nose and exhale slowly through your mouth. Take normal breaths, not deep ones.

- While you exhale, say the relaxing word you have chosen. Say it very slowly, like this, "c-a-a-a-a-a-a-l-m" or "r-e-e-e-l-a-a-a-x."

- Pause after exhaling before taking your next breath. If it's not too distracting, count to four before inhaling each new breath.

- Repeat the entire sequence 10 to 15 times.

Muscle relaxation

The goal of this technique is to gently stretch your muscles to reduce stiffness and tension. The exercises start at your head and work down to your feet. You can do these exercises while sitting in a chair.

Steps:

- Shoulder shrugs. Lift both shoulders in a shrugging motion. Try to touch your ears with your shoulders. Let your shoulders drop down after each shrug. Repeat 3-5 times.

- Overhead arm stretches*. Raise both arms straight above your head. Interlace your fingers, like you're making a basket, with your palms facing down (towards the floor). Stretch your arms towards the ceiling. Then, keeping your fingers interlaced, rotate your palms to face upwards (towards the ceiling). Stretch towards the ceiling. Repeat 3-5 times.

- Stomach tension. Pull your stomach muscles toward your back as tight as you can tolerate. Feel the tension and hold on to it for ten seconds. Then let go of the muscles and let your stomach relax, further and further. Then focus on the release from the tension. Notice the heavy yet comfortable sensation in your stomach.

- Knee raises. Reach down and grab your right knee with one or both hands. Pull your knee up towards your chest (as close to your chest as is comfortable). Hold your knee there for a few seconds, before returning your foot to the floor.

Reach down and grab your left knee with one or both hands and bring it up towards your chest. Hold it there for a few seconds. Repeat the sequence 3-5 times.

- <u>Foot and ankle rolls</u>. Lift your feet and stretch your legs out. Rotate your ankles and feet, 3-5 times in one direction, then 3-5 times in the other direction.

*If it is not comfortable to do step #2 with your arms overhead, try it with your arms reaching out in front of you.

Imagining a peaceful scene

The goal of this technique is to "take yourself away" from stress and picture yourself in a more relaxed, calm situation.

Steps:

1. Choose a scene that you find peaceful, calm and restful. If you have trouble thinking of a scene, consider the following:

    - at the beach
    - on a walk in the woods
    - on a park bench
    - on a mountain path
    - in a canoe or sailboat
    - in a meadow
    - traveling on a train
    - in a cabin
    - beside a river
    - next to a waterfall
    - in a high rise apartment overlooking a large city
    - riding a bicycle
    - on a farm

2. After choosing a peaceful scene, imagine as many details as possible, using all your senses.

3. What does the scene look like? What are the colors? Is it light or dark? What shapes are in the scene? If it's a nature scene, what kinds of trees or flowers do you see? What animals? If it's a city scene, what kind of buildings? What kind of vehicles?

4. What sounds are in your peaceful scene? Can you hear water or the sounds of waves? Are there sounds from animals or birds? From the breeze? From people?

5. What could you feel with your sense of touch? Are there textures? Is it cool or warm? Can you feel a breeze?

6. What smells are there in your peaceful scene? Could you smell flowers? The smell of the ocean? The smell of food cooking?

7. Disregard any stressful thoughts and keep your attention on the peaceful scene.

8. Allow at least five minutes for this relaxation technique.

Coping with Problems and Symptoms

CHAPTER 9

Introduction

This handout describes strategies for coping with common problems and persistent symptoms. People sometimes experience stress due to depression, anxiety, sleep problems, hearing voices, and other symptoms. Coping strategies can be effective at reducing symptoms or distress related to symptoms. Other strategies can be used to deal with day-to-day problems encountered in living.

The importance of coping with problems

Problems are a natural part of life. Everyone encounters some problems along the way, no matter how well they are managing their lives. Some problems are easily solved and cause very little stress. Other problems are more challenging, and can result in significant stress. When stress builds up, it can cause persistent symptoms to worsen and can lead to a relapse.

This handout will provide a step-by-step method for solving problems and achieving goals. It will also provide some specific strategies for coping with problems that people commonly encounter, including problems related to persistent psychiatric symptoms.

> *Developing strategies for coping with problems can help reduce stress.*

Question: What is an example of a problem that has caused you stress?

A step-by-step method for solving problems and achieving goals

When trying to solve a problem or achieve a goal, it is important to take an active, solution-focused approach. The following structured, step-by-step method was introduced in the handout "Recovery Strategies." This method can be used for solving problems caused by persistent symptoms and achieving goals by yourself or with members of your support system, such as family members, friends, peers, or practitioners. These people can be especially helpful in contributing ideas for solutions and in carrying out specific steps of the solution you choose.

Step-By-Step Problem-Solving and Goal Achievement

Step 1. Define the problem or the goal you would like to achieve. Be as specific as possible.

Step 2. List some possible solutions (at least 3). This step is for brainstorming. Don't evaluate whether the solutions are good or bad yet.

Step 3. For each solution, list one advantage (pro) and one disadvantage (con). Be brief, but give each solution a chance.

Step 4. Choose the best solution or combination of solutions. Which solution is most likely to solve the problem or achieve the goal? Which solution can be realistically carried out?

Step 5. Plan how to carry out the solution. Answer these questions:
Who will be involved in carrying out the solution?
What step will each person do?
What is the time frame for each step?
What resources are needed?
What obstacles might come up and how could they be overcome?

Step 6. Set a date for evaluating how the solution is working. First focus on the positive: What has been accomplished? What went well? Then decide if the solution was successful or if you need to revise it or choose another one.

The more you use this method for solving problems and achieving goals, the easier and smoother it will become.

> *Using a step-by-step method for solving problems and achieving goals can help you take an active, solution-focused approach.*

<u>Questions</u>: Are you experiencing a problem that is causing stress? Or is there a goal that you would like to achieve but is difficult to pursue?
You can use the following worksheet(s) to develop a plan for solving the problem or achieving the goal.

Step-by-Step Problem-Solving and Goal Achievement

1. Define the problem or goal as specifically and simply as possible.

2. List 3 possible ways to solve the problem or achieve the goal:
   a.
   b.
   c.

3. For each possibility, list one advantage and one disadvantage:
   <u>Advantages/pros</u>:   <u>Disadvantages/cons</u>:
   a.   a.
   b.   b.
   c.   c.

4. Choose the best way to solve the problem or achieve the goal. Which way has the best chance of succeeding?

5. Plan the steps for carrying out the solution. Who will be involved? What step will each person do? What is the time frame? What resources are needed? What problems might come up? How could they be overcome?
   a.
   b.
   c.
   d.
   e.
   f.

6. Set a date for follow up: _____. Give yourself credit for what you have done. Decide whether the problem has been solved or whether the goal has been achieved. If not, decide whether to revise the plan or try another one.

Step-by-Step Problem-Solving and Goal Achievement

1. Define the problem or goal as specifically and simply as possible.

2. List 3 possible ways to solve the problem or achieve the goal:
   a.
   b.
   c.

3. For each possibility, list one advantage and one disadvantage:
   <u>Advantages/pros</u>:   <u>Disadvantages/cons</u>
   a.   a.
   b.   b.
   c.   c.

4. Choose the best way to solve the problem or achieve the goal. Which way has the best chance of succeeding?

5. Plan the steps for carrying out the solution. Who will be involved? What step will each person do? What is the time frame? What resources are needed? What problems might come up? How could they be overcome?
   a.
   b.
   c.
   d.
   e.
   f.

6. Set a date for follow up:_____. Give yourself credit for what you have done. Decide whether the problem has been solved or whether the goal has been achieved. If not, decide whether to revise the plan or try another one.

Common problems

The rest of this handout will focus on some of the problems that people commonly encounter, including problems related to persistent psychiatric symptoms. When these problems are not addressed, they can cause distress, contribute to stress, and increase the risk of relapse.

Persistent symptoms

What do we mean by persistent symptoms? Some symptoms of a psychiatric illness occur much of the time, although their strength may vary over time. Many people have some form of persistent symptoms. Common ones include distressing anxiety, hearing voices, depression, and having suspicious thoughts about others. Persistent symptoms can be distressing and at times may get in the way of your enjoyment of life. This module will teach strategies for coping with persistent symptoms so people can pursue important personal goals and have a good quality of life in spite of experiencing symptoms that may not go away.

While persistent symptoms usually do not signal an approaching crisis, it is important to know that occasionally a persistent symptom can change or worsen to the point of becoming an early warning sign of relapse.

Being able to tell the difference between a persistent symptom and an early warning sign of relapse is not always easy. Warning signs are symptoms that tend to come before a relapse such as disturbed sleep or eating patterns, increased isolation or intrusive behavior towards others, or a considerable worsening of usual symptoms. In contrast, persistent symptoms are more constant and usually have not led to past relapses. Working together with staff members and other important people in your life to help you recognize the difference between these two types of symptoms is an important skill. This module will concentrate on ways to manage persistent symptoms and other problems. (Strategies for dealing with early warning signs are discussed in Module 6, "Reducing Relapses".)

Because each person is an individual, no one has the same set of problems. In order to develop coping strategies that work for you, it is helpful to first identify the specific problems you have experienced. You can use the following checklist to help in this process:

Checklist of Common Problems and Persistent Symptoms

Category of problem	Specific problem	I experience this problem
Thinking problems	paying attention	
	concentrating	
Mood problems	anxiety	
	depression	
	anger	
	sleeping difficulties	
Negative symptoms	lack of interest	
	lack of pleasure	
	lack of expressiveness	
	social withdrawal	
Psychotic symptoms	hallucinations	
	delusions	
Drug and alcohol use	drugs	
	alcohol	
	other substances	
Other problem area:		

> *People often experience problems or persistent symptoms in the following categories:*
>
> - *thinking*
> - *mood*
> - *negative symptoms*
> - *psychotic symptoms*
> - *abusing drugs or alcohol*

Questions: Which of these common problems or persistent symptoms do you experience? Which one causes the most stress for you?

Strategies for coping with specific problems and persistent symptoms

Several coping strategies are suggested for each problem listed in the Common Problem and Persistent Symptom Checklist to enable you to pick and choose the strategies that you think might work for you. Next to each strategy is a box that you can check off to indicate that you would like to try the strategy.

It is important to keep in mind that if any of the following problems described begin to worsen or interfere significantly with your life, they may be signs of an impending relapse. In such situations, it is suggested that you contact your doctor or practitioner to help you evaluate what steps to take.

> *There are a variety of strategies for coping with problems and persistent symptoms. It's important to choose the ones that you think will help you the most.*

Thinking problems

Please check off the strategy that you would like to try.

Concentration

Sometimes people have problems concentrating on conversations or activities. The following strategies may be helpful:

- Minimize distractions, so there is only one thing to concentrate on. For example, if you're trying to concentrate on a phone conversation, make sure the radio and TV are off, and that other people aren't talking nearby.
- Ask the person with whom you are conversing to slow down or repeat things that you're unsure of.
- Check to make sure you understand by summarizing what you heard. For example, you can say something like, "Let me see if I understand your main point; are you saying_____?"
- Break down activities or tasks into smaller parts, and take frequent breaks. For example, if you have to clean your apartment, you could try breaking the task down into one room at a time, taking breaks between each room. You could break it down further, by cleaning only one section of each room at a time. For example, in the kitchen you could start with the sink area, and then move to the stove area.

Attention

- Choose an interesting activity that requires attention, but start out by spending a brief time on the activity and gradually increasing the amount of time. For example, if you are having difficulty paying attention when reading, you could start by reading a few paragraphs of an article in a newspaper or magazine. When you feel comfortable with that, you could try selecting a short article and reading it entirely. In this way, you could gradually build up to reading chapters in a book.   The important thing is to progress at a pace that's comfortable for you.
- Ask someone to join you in an activity that requires attention, such as a board game, card game, or a jigsaw puzzle. Many people find that doing something together helps them focus better.

Questions: Which of the strategies did you identify that you would like to try?
How could you put one or more of the strategies into practice? You can use the following chart to record your answer:

Plan for Coping with Thinking Problems

Strategy I would like to try	When I would like to try it	Steps I will take

Mood problems

Please check off the strategies that you would like to try.

Anxiety

When people are anxious, they usually feel worried, nervous, or afraid. There are often physical signs of anxiety, such as muscle tension, headaches, heart racing, or shortness of breath. People may feel anxious about certain situations and go to extremes to avoid them. Some strategies for coping with anxiety are listed below:

- Talk with someone in your support system to let him or her know about your feelings.
- Use relaxation techniques, such as deep breathing or progressive muscle relaxation, to stay calm.
- Identify situations that tend to make you anxious and making a plan to do something about them. For example, if you are anxious about an upcoming application deadline, make plans to start working on the first part of the application.
- Work with your practitioner on a plan for <u>gradually</u> exposing yourself to situations that makes you feel anxious.
  For example, if someone is anxious about taking the bus, he or she might start by waiting at the bus stop and watching people get on and off the bus. After becoming more comfortable with that, he or she might try getting on the bus and getting off at the first stop. The idea is to feel comfortable before moving on to the next step.

Depression

When people are depressed, they may have one or more of the following problems: feeling bad about themselves, not doing the things they used to enjoy, sleeping too much or too little, low energy, poor appetite, and having trouble concentrating and making decisions.

If you get severely depressed or if you start thinking of hurting yourself or ending your life, you should contact your practitioner immediately or seek emergency services. However, if you are not having severe symptoms of depression, you can try the following coping strategies to help improve your mood:

- Set goals for daily activities, starting with one or two activities and gradually building up to a full schedule.
- Identify things that you still enjoy and build your strengths in those areas.
- Schedule something pleasant to do each day, even if it's a small thing. This will give you something to look forward to.
- Talk to someone in your support system to let him or her know how you're feeling. Sometimes they have good ideas you can try.
- Ask people to join you in activities. You may be more likely to follow through with plans when someone else is involved.
- Deal with loss of appetite by eating small portions of food that you like and taking your time.
- Practice relaxation exercises on a regular basis.
- Remind yourself of the steps you have accomplished and avoid focusing on setbacks.

Anger

Some people find that they feel angry or irritable much of the time and get outraged about situations that would ordinarily seem relatively minor.

Because this is a common problem, there are programs for anger management, which many people have found helpful. Some of the techniques taught in anger management classes include:

- Recognize the <u>early</u> signs that you are starting to feel angry (for example, heart pounding, jaw clenching, perspiring), so that you can keep things from getting out of control.
- Identify situations that commonly make you feel angry and learn how to handle these situations more effectively.
- Develop strategies for staying calm when you're angry, such as counting to ten before responding, distracting yourself, temporarily leaving the situation, or politely changing the subject.
- Learn how to express angry feelings briefly and constructively. The following steps are helpful:
- Speak firmly but calmly.
- Tell the person what he or she did to upset you. Be brief.
- Suggest how the situation could be avoided in the future.

Sleeping difficulties

Sleeping too much or too little can be very disruptive. It's hard to accomplish things when you don't get enough sleep.

Trying some of the following strategies may help:

- Go to sleep and get up at the same time every day.
- Avoid caffeine after 6 PM.
- Exercise during the day so you'll feel tired at night.
- Do something relaxing before going to bed, such as reading, taking a warm shower, drinking warm milk or herbal tea, or listening to music
- Make sure that your room is dark and that the temperature is comfortable.
- Avoid watching violent or distressing programs on television or video just before going to bed.
- Avoid having discussions about upsetting topics just before going to bed.
- Avoid napping during the day.
- Avoid spending more than 30 minutes lying awake in bed. Instead, try getting up, going to another room, and doing something relaxing (like reading or listening to music) for at least 15 minutes before returning to bed.

Questions: Which of the strategies did you identify that you would like to try? How could you put one or more of the strategies into practice? You can use the following chart to record your answer:

Plan for Coping with Mood Problems

Strategy I would like to try	When I would like to try it	Steps I will take

Negative symptoms

Please check off the strategies that you would like to try.

Lack of interest and lack of pleasure

It's very difficult to stay active when things don't seem interesting to you or when you don't enjoy things you used to enjoy. It's also difficult to pursue goals when you feel this way.

The following strategies may be helpful to gradually increase your interest and enjoyment of activities:

- Be patient with yourself. Changes will happen gradually.
- Start with an activity that you used to enjoy. Think of something brief that you could do that is related to that activity. For example, if you used to enjoy jogging, you could try taking a brief walk (5-10 minutes) in the neighborhood. Be attentive to what you experience as you walk: What do you see? What do you hear? What do you smell? How does your body feel being active? Do you feel more relaxed after walking?
- As you gain more confidence in brief activities, gradually plan longer activities. For example, after taking short daily walks in your neighborhood for a few weeks, you could try taking a walk to an interesting place (a park or shopping area) further away. Or you might try staying in the neighborhood, but walking at a slightly faster pace. After several weeks, you might gradually work up to taking a short jog.

- Ask people in your support system to do things with you. It can be more enjoyable to have someone with whom to converse and share the experience. For example, when you take a walk with a friend or family member it becomes a social experience as well as a physical one.
- Regularly schedule enjoyable activities. For example, you could set up a schedule of walking every morning after breakfast. The more regularly you do an activity, the more likely you will start to feel enjoyment in it.
- Investigate new interests such as the following:
    - Computers (games, e-mail, websites, chat rooms, word processing, etc.)
    - Doing artwork or crafts
    - Visiting museums (art, science, natural history, history)
    - Games (chess, checkers, cards, etc.)
    - Collecting coins or stamps
    - Cooking (different varieties such as microwave specialties, Chinese, Italian, French, cookies, cakes, etc)
    - Exercising (bicycling, swimming, calisthenics, aerobics, dance-based exercises)
    - Gardening (indoor or outdoor)
    - Walking
    - Running
    - Humor (reading jokes, telling jokes to others, humorous movies or television shows)
    - Listening to music
    - Playing a musical instrument
    - Watching sports (at the event or on television)
    - Playing sports
    - Reading (fiction, non-fiction, humor, mysteries, poetry, plays)

- Writing (journal, poetry, newsletter, articles, stories, novels)
- Yoga (class or video)
- Singing (by yourself or with others)
- Nature (books, videos, television shows about nature)
- Playing musical instruments
- Science-related interests (astronomy, math, weather)
- Word games (crossword puzzles, Scrabble, Wheel of Fortune, Password, Pictionary, word scrambles)
- Trivia/Knowledge games (Trivial Pursuit, Jeopardy, Name that Tune, Tripod)
- Sewing, knitting
- Other:
- Other:

❏ Be willing to try something several times in order to get familiar with it. The more familiar and comfortable you feel with an activity, the more likely you will enjoy it.

Lack of expressiveness

If other people tell you that they cannot read your facial expression or that it is hard to tell what you are thinking or feeling by your expression or tone of voice, it may indicate that you are having a problem with expressing your emotions. This can create misunderstandings. For example, when you are interested in something, other people may think you are bored or not paying attention. The following strategies may help you avoid this kind of misunderstanding:

- Verbally express what you are feeling or thinking. Make frequent clear comments about your reactions to conversations or activities.
- Make "I" statements that clearly express your point of view or your feelings, such as the following:

  - "I'm enjoying talking to you today. You are lifting my spirits."
  - "I was a little nervous about playing ping pong today. But I'm glad I did, because it was fun."
  - "I liked that movie because it was funny."
  - "I'm feeling a little discouraged today."

Social Withdrawal

Everyone needs time alone. But if you find that you are withdrawing from people and avoiding contact with others, it may create problems in your relationships. The following strategies may be helpful in coping with social withdrawal:

- Join a support group.
- Explore jobs or volunteer work that involve
- contact with other people.
- Schedule contact with someone every day, even if it's for a short time.
- If you find it stressful to be with people, practice relaxation techniques (see the handout "Coping
- with Stress") before and/or after your contact with them.
- If it's too stressful to have personal contact, call people on the phone and talk for at least a few minutes.
- Arrange for errands that involve contact with people, such as going to the store or the library.
- Make a list of people in your support system with whom you feel most comfortable. Call them when you are feeling that you are starting to withdraw. If possible, make a plan to meet with them.
- Sometimes it's more comfortable to spend time with people when doing an activity together. Try planning activities with someone, such as going to museums or a musical performance.

Questions: Which of the strategies did you identify that you would like to try?
How could you put one or more of the strategies into practice? You can use the following chart to record your answer:

Plan for Coping with Problems Related to Negative Symptoms

Strategy I would like to try	When I would like to try it	Steps I will take

Psychotic symptoms

Please check off the strategies you would like to try.

Delusions

Sometimes people develop beliefs that are firmly held in spite of contradictory evidence. For example, they might start to believe that the FBI is monitoring their phone calls even though there is no evidence of this. Or they might believe that people are talking about them or staring at them. For some people having this kind of belief, which is called a "delusion," is an early sign that they are starting to experience a relapse of their mental illness, and they need to contact their practitioner to discuss an evaluation.

For some people, however, these kinds of beliefs do not go away between episodes of their illness, and unless they get worse than usual, they are not necessarily a sign that an evaluation is needed.
If this is your situation, such beliefs may be distressing or distracting, however, and you might try one or more of the following coping strategies:

- ❑ Distract yourself from the disturbing belief by doing something that takes your mental attention, such as doing a puzzle or adding up rows of numbers.
- ❑ Check out your beliefs by talking to someone you trust. For example, you might ask your practitioner to help you evaluate the evidence for and against your belief. Ask for his or her point of view. If your beliefs cause you to worry about safety, for example, you might ask, "What is

the evidence that supports that I am in danger, and what is the evidence that does not support that I am in danger?"
- Distract yourself with a physical activity, like going for a brisk walk.

If you try the strategies listed above, but still feel distressed or distracted by beliefs, it may be helpful to mention it to someone in your support system. You may also benefit from consulting the Relapse Prevention Plan you developed in the handout "Reducing Relapses."

Keep in mind that you should contact your practitioner if you become so convinced of your belief that you are thinking of acting on it. For example, if you become convinced that someone means you harm, you might start thinking of defending yourself, which could possibly lead you to harm someone else. If you can't reach you practitioner, seek out emergency services under these circumstances.

Hallucinations

Sometimes people hear voices or see things when nothing is there. They might even feel, taste, or smell something when nothing is there. These experiences are called "false perceptions" or "hallucinations." For some people, when this happens it is a sign that they are starting to experience a relapse of their mental illness and should contact their practitioner to discuss an evaluation.

For some people, however, these hallucinations do not go away between episodes, and unless they get worse than usual they are not necessarily a sign that an evaluation is needed. If this is your situation, you may find it distressing or distracting, however, and you might want to try one or more of the following coping strategies:

- Distract yourself by doing something that takes your attention, such as having a conversation with someone, reading, or taking a walk. Some people who hear voices hum to themselves or listen to a Walkman to drown out voices.
- Check out your experiences with someone you trust. For example, one person who thought he heard voices outside his window asked his brother to listen and give an opinion.
- Use positive self-talk. Some people tell themselves things like, "I'm not going to listen to these voices," or "I'm not going to let these voices get to me," or "I'm just going to stay cool and the situation will pass."

- Ignore the hallucinations as much as possible. Some people say that it helps to focus on other things instead.

- Put the hallucinations "in the background." Some people say they acknowledge what they are hearing or seeing, but don't pay any further attention to it. For example, they might tell themselves, "There's that critical voice again. I'm just going to let it happen and go about my business. I'm not going to let it bother me or affect what I'm doing."
- Use relaxation techniques. Some people find that the voices or visual hallucinations get worse when they are under stress. Doing some deep breathing or muscle relaxation reduces the stress and reduces some of the intensity of the hallucination. (See the Appendix of the handout "Coping with Stress" for examples of relaxation techniques.)

If the voices start to tell you to do something to hurt yourself or someone else and you think you might act on this, however, you need to contact your practitioner or emergency services.

Questions: Which of the strategies did you identify that you would like to try? How could you put one or more of the strategies into practice? You can use the following chart to record your answer:

Plan for Coping with Problems Related to Psychotic Symptoms

Strategy I would like to try	When I would like to try it	Steps I will take

Drug or alcohol abuse problems

If you are experiencing problems with alcohol, drugs, or over-the-counter medications, you are not alone. These problems are called "substance abuse," and are very common, affecting people from all walks of life. It's especially common for people with mental illness to have problems with alcohol or drug use. If someone has both a mental illness and a substance abuse problem, the two disorders are often referred to as "dual disorders" or "dual diagnosis."

Drugs and alcohol can make the symptoms of mental illness worse and can interfere with the benefits of prescribed medication. To stay well, therefore, it is very important to address any problems you might have with drugs or alcohol.

The coping strategies described below can be very helpful, but it is important to keep in mind that most people need additional help to overcome serious alcohol or drug problems. Programs that integrate treatment for mental illness with treatment for substance abuse have the most positive results. Self-help programs such as AA (Alcoholics Anonymous), NA (Narcotics Anonymous), Dual Recovery and Double Trouble (for people with both substance abuse and mental illness) are also extremely helpful.

Whether or not you are participating in an integrated treatment program or a self-help group, it is important to develop strategies that you can use for dealing with drug or alcohol problems.

Please check off the strategies that you would like to try:
(Most of these strategies are also discussed in Educational Handout #6 in this program; "Drug and Alcohol Use.)

- ❑ Educate yourself about the scientific facts about drugs and alcohol. For example, it is helpful to know that although alcohol in small amounts may be relaxing, it can also cause depression. Also, people with mental illness are more sensitive to the effects of drugs and alcohol, resulting in problems associated with using even small or moderate amounts of drugs or alcohol. These substances also make your prescribed medication less effective.
- ❑ Identify the advantages and disadvantages of using drugs or alcohol. What are the things that you like about using drugs or alcohol? What are the things that you don't like about it?
  Some of the advantages people report include, "I like smoking marijuana because it's fun to do with friends," or "I sleep better after I've been smoking." On the other hand, they report disadvantages such as, "Smoking pot makes me paranoid," and "I spend all my money when I go out smoking and have nothing left to pay the rent."
- ❑ Be realistic about how using drugs and/or alcohol has affected your life. For some people, the effects may be relatively minor, like having less spending money. For others the effects are more extensive, like losing friends, having legal problems, being unable to keep a job.
- ❑ Develop alternatives to using drugs or alcohol. What are other ways of getting some of the positive effects that you look for when using drugs or alcohol? What are some other ways of getting your needs met? For example, some people report the following alternatives: "I signed up for a class in

photography so I would have something else to do with my time" and "Doing some kind of exercise makes me feel less depressed—without the hangover."
- Practice how to respond to people who offer you drugs or alcohol. Some examples of possible responses include:
    - "When I see Thomas coming, I go the other way, because he always wants to get high with me."
    - "I tell people I'm on my way someplace else and can't stop."
    - "I tell Alberto that I want to spend time with him, but I'd rather go to a movie."
    - "I have to be direct with Maria and say, 'I don't drink anymore so don't ask me to go to the bar with you.'"
    - "If one of those pushers tries to come up to me on the street, I just walk by quickly and don't make eye contact."
- Keep in mind the advantages of avoiding drugs and alcohol. To strengthen their determination, some people keep a list such as the following:
    - I'll be able to save money.
    - I'll be less depressed in the long run.
    - I'll stay out of the hospital.
    - I'll be able to keep my job.
    - I won't have as many arguments with my family.
    - I'll feel better physically.

<u>Questions:</u> What strategies did you identify that you would like to try?

How could you put one or more of the strategies into practice? You can use the following chart to record your answer:

Plan for Coping with Problems Related to Drug or Alcohol Abuse

Strategy I would like to try	When I would like to try it	Steps I will take

Examples of people using coping strategies

Example #1

"I enjoy watching football on TV, but I can't concentrate for the length of a whole game. So I usually videotape the game. I can fast-forward the tape past the commercials, which cuts down the time. I can also turn it off and take a break whenever I want. It works well for me."

Example #2

"When I feel depressed, I tend to dwell on all my failures. It helps me to call my sister, who always reminds me of what I've accomplished. Talking to her makes me feel better about the future."

Example #3

"I sometimes have a problem with anger. I hold it inside and it builds up. It's better for me to express my feelings and get them off my chest. I stay calm, though, and keep it short and simple."

Example #4

"I was having trouble getting interested in things. I was just sitting in my apartment all day. I've decided to get involved in one of my old hobbies, photography. I used to really enjoy taking pictures. To get started I went to a photography exhibit at the museum. And I'm sorting through some old family photographs to organize them into an album. It's bringing back some of my old interest. I'm thinking about taking a class."

Example #5

"Even though I'm taking medications, I still hear voices. Sometimes they are loud and say disturbing things. I use a couple of strategies for this. Sometimes I listen to music on my headphones. It helps to drown out the voices. Sometimes I walk to the park and shoot a few baskets. It helps distract me from the voices."

Example #6

"I used to smoke marijuana in the evening when I was bored. But every time I smoked it caused my symptoms to get worse. So now I try to schedule activities in the evening so I don't get bored. For example, I'm taking a class in computers, which I don't know anything about. It's keeping me from thinking about marijuana for now."

Plan for coping with problems and persistent symptoms

This handout included several checklists and planning sheets to help you identify coping strategies for specific problems and persistent symptoms. Completing the following chart, "Plan for Coping with Problems and Persistent Symptoms" will help you summarize that information.

> *It is helpful to have a plan for putting coping strategies into action.*

Plan for Coping with Problems and Persistent Symptoms

Problem or Symptoms	Strategy I plan to use

Summary of the main points about coping with problems and persistent symptoms

- *Developing strategies for coping with problems and persistent symptoms can help reduce stress.*

- *Using a step-by-step method for solving problems and achieving goals can help you take an active, solution-focused approach.*

- *People often experience problems in the following categories:*

  - *Thinking*
  - *Mood*
  - *Negative symptoms*
  - *Psychotic symptoms*
  - *Abusing drugs or alcohol*

- *There are a variety of strategies for coping with problems and persistent symptoms. It is important to choose the ones that you think will help you the most.*

- *It is helpful to have a plan for putting coping strategies into action.*

Getting Your Needs Met in the Mental Health System

CHAPTER 10

Introduction

This handout provides an overview of the mental health system, including the services and programs available at many mental health centers. Information is provided to help people evaluate what programs they might like to participate in to further their own recovery. Strategies are provided to help people advocate effectively for themselves when they encounter a problem in the mental health system.

What are community mental health centers?

In the United States, Community Mental Health Centers (CMHCs) are the main source of public outpatient mental health services. In some states, the CMHCs provide services only to people who live in a certain geographic area. In other states, you may have a choice as to which CMHC you want to receive services from. Rates for services vary. People are charged based on insurance coverage, eligibility for medical assistance, and income.

It is important to keep in mind that in many states the mental health system is in the process of making extensive changes. For example, some public mental health services are now being provided by managed care organizations. Some of the changes may result in confusion about which services are being offered, who is eligible, and how to get access. Case managers and social workers usually have current information.

Psychiatrists and therapists are also available in the private sector, including private agencies, local hospitals, teaching hospitals, counseling agencies, and some employment programs. Private insurance and/or financial resources may be necessary to afford these services. However, some organizations, such as teaching hospitals, have special programs for providing mental health services that are more affordable.

> *Community Mental Health Centers are the main source of public outpatient mental health services.*

What are some of the types of services offered by Community Mental Health Centers?

Community Mental Health Centers (or agencies that are affiliated with them) usually provide a wide range of services. If they do not provide the services you are looking for, they may be able to give you information on where to find them in your community. Your center may provide some of the following:

- Mental health evaluations
- case management
- medication services
- peer support or other consumer-led programs
- individual therapy
- group therapy

- social skills training
- family psychoeducation and other family services
- day treatment programs or partial hospital programs
- support groups
- education about mental illness
- emergency services
- occupational therapy
- recreational therapy
- employment services
- integrated mental health and substance use treatment
- access to Assertive Community Treatment Teams (ACT Teams)

Community Mental Health Centers usually provide a wide range of services.

Which services might be helpful to you?

The needs of people with psychiatric symptoms differ from one person to the next. Mental health centers often offer a variety of services to meet each person's needs.

You may have already used some of the following services and may be interested in trying others. As you read the following descriptions of other people's experiences, please check off the services that you would like to try.

- **Mental Health Evaluation**

"It helped me to have a complete mental health assessment. I had been having problems for a while and going from one bad experience to another. I talked with the psychologist doing the assessment about the problems I'd been having. He also asked questions about what was going well in my life, what I'm good at, and what kind of support I have. It gave me a better perspective."

- **Case Management**

"I work closely with my case manager. When I need it, he helps me with all kinds of practical things, like helping me to apply for benefits and arranging for free transportation to my appointments. He also helped me find out what I needed to get involved in a supported employment program. He really knows the mental health system in and out."

- **Medication services**

"My doctor helped me to find the medication that I'm taking now. I tried a few kinds before I settled on this one. My doctor had a lot of experience, which really helped. Now I see her once a month."

- **Peer support/consumer-led programs**

"Going to a recovery program which was designed and led by people who had experienced psychiatric symptoms themselves was a key ingredient to my recovery. I got a chance to be with people who really understood me. I've also gotten a chance to help other people. It makes me feel much more confident and optimistic about the future."

- <u>Individual therapy</u>

"Having someone I can talk to about issues in my life is really important to me. My counselor helped me to sort out some problems I was having in my relationship with my boyfriend. She also encouraged me to go back to school, which I'm currently considering."

- <u>Group therapy</u>

"In my therapy group we talk about our feelings and different ways to cope with situations that come up in our lives. I feel comfortable talking with the people in the group about what's on my mind."

- <u>Social skills training</u>

"I've learned a lot in my Social Skills Training group. I had been having trouble making friends, and being in the group taught me how to start conversations and keep it going. It also gave me a chance to try conversations in the group before I tried it at my job. The feedback from the other group members has been very helpful."

- <u>Family psychoeducation and other family services</u>

"I asked my Mom and Dad and brother to sign up with me for a family psychoeducation group at the Mental Health Center. It really helped to have them learn more about my illness. And it made us better able to talk together."

- **Day treatment or partial hospitalization program**

"I feel better when I have some structure every day. I like seeing people I know and having something to do. We have educational groups and leisure groups. I especially like the music groups."

- **Housing Options**

"I'm living in an apartment building that is owned by the Community Mental Health Center. I have my own apartment, but there is always a staff member around to help me if I need it. I like the other people in the building."

- **Support groups**

"Hearing from other people who have gone through similar things is very helpful to me. I don't feel like I'm the only one. And the other people have good ideas that I can try out."

- **Emergency services**

"My mental health center has a 24 hour crisis line. I used it once when I was under a lot of stress, and it helped me stay in control."

- **Occupational therapy (O.T.)**

"Working with the occupational therapist helped me to get myself organized with shopping and cooking. Before that I was eating out all the time, which was really expensive."

- <u>Recreational Therapy (R.T.)</u>

"The recreational therapist helped me to get involved with my hobbies again. He encouraged me to get out my guitar and practice some songs. It's been great to play music again."

- <u>Integrated mental health and substance use treatment</u>

"I used to get confused because my drug counselor told me one thing, and my mental health counselor told me another. Now we're all working together and I'm making progress."

- <u>Employment services</u>

"I'm starting part-time work next week at a book store. The supported employment specialist asked me what kind of work I had done in the past and what I was interested in doing now. She helped me find a job that suited me. Now she's going to stay involved while I'm working. I feel like I've got support for going back to work."

- <u>Assertive Community Treatment Team (ACT Team)</u>

"I used to be in and out of the hospital all the time. Now I have an ACT Team who helps me stay in the community. They help me with all kinds of things, including housing and transportation."

> *Individuals vary widely in the mental health services they use.*

Question: Which mental health services did you check off that you would like to try? You can record your answers on the following checklist:

Mental Health Services Checklist

Service	I would like to try this service
Mental health evaluation	
Case management	
Medication services	
Peer support/consumer-led programs	
Individual therapy	
Group therapy	
Social skills training	
Family psychoeducation and other family services	
Day treatment/partial hospitalization programs	
Housing options	
Support groups	
Emergency services	
Occupational therapy	
Recreational therapy	
Integrated treatment for mental health and substance use	
Employment services	
Assertive Community Treatment (ACT)	
Other:	

How can you find out more about what is involved in participating in specific programs?

You may find out information about the key parts of these services from the community mental health centers, mental health research centers, consumer support agencies, and from advocacy groups. Some information is available on websites, and some can be found by checking your local phone book or by calling the offices of your state or county division of mental health.

Are you entitled to financial benefits?

Benefit programs are established to help members of our community when they are having financial difficulties. Sometimes people do not apply for these programs because they feel a sense of embarrassment attached to them. It is important to remember that you are part of a larger community and deserve to receive the financial and other supports that are intended to help people manage their lives.

Understanding and applying for benefits can be a complicated task. Talking with a case manager or social worker is a good way to find out what benefits you may be entitled to and how to apply for them. A case manager or social worker will also know of any recent changes in benefit programs.

Depending on your work history and current financial needs, you may qualify for one of the following financial benefits:

Social Security Disability Insurance (SSDI)

If you worked in the past and contributed to Social Security (or your disability started before you reached the age of eighteen) and are currently unable to work full-time because of mental illness, you may be eligible for SSDI. It is a federal program, and you can apply for it at the Social Security Administration Office. After two years of being eligible for SSDI, you might be eligible for Medicare health insurance.

Supplemental Security Income (SSI)

If you have not worked in the past (or are only eligible for a small amount of SSDI), are currently unable to work full-time because of mental illness, and have very limited financial resources, you may be eligible for Supplemental Security Income (SSI). It is a federal program, and you can apply at the Social Security Administration Office. If you receive SSI you may also be eligible for Medicaid health insurance.

Public Assistance

Each state offers different financial benefits and has different eligibility requirements. State benefit programs are often called "public assistance" or "temporary assistance for needy families" or "welfare programs." If you have a low income and have mental health problems that interfere with working full-time, you may be eligible for public assistance. It is usually a modest amount of money.

Many states also have programs to assist with the purchase of food, such as food stamps. Many states and communities have programs to help with housing costs. The housing programs may be operated by local housing authorities or by the states.

Because public assistance is funded by the state, you would apply at the state Office of Public Assistance or Office of Public Welfare. You may also be eligible for Medicaid health insurance, which is sometimes called "medical assistance."

> *Depending on your work history and financial need, you may be eligible for SSI, SSDI or Public Assistance.*

Questions: Are you currently receiving financial benefits?
If not, do you think you might be eligible for SSDI, SSI or Public Assistance?

Are you entitled to health insurance benefits?

Social workers and case managers are usually well informed about health insurance benefits. The details about these benefits may vary from year to year, so it's a good idea to start by talking to someone who knows the most recent information.

You may be eligible for one of the following health care benefits:

Medicare

If you are unable to work full-time because of mental illness and have been eligible to receive SSDI for more than two years, you may be eligible for Medicare. It usually covers inpatient and outpatient bills, although it is subject to deductibles, co-payments and "ceilings" for certain services. Medicare has two programs, Medicare A and Medicare B. You can get information about these programs from your local Social Security Office. Even if you are not sure that you will receive Medicare or Social Security, you have the right to apply. Applications are made at the Social Security Administration Office.

Medicaid

If you have a low income (or no income) and have mental health problems that interfere with working full-time, you may be eligible for Medicaid, which is called "Medical Assistance" in some states. Even though the programs vary from state to state, they usually cover inpatient and outpatient bills, and medication costs. In some states you are required to pay small co-payments and there are restrictions on reimbursements. You can apply at the State Office of Public Assistance or Office of Public Welfare.

Appealing Decisions

The Social Security Administration and local state programs (such as Medicaid) have ways that you can appeal decisions that have been made about whether you are eligible for services. When you apply, ask about what the appeal process is. If you feel a decision was not made correctly, you have a right to follow the appeal process.

Depending on your work history and financial need, you may be eligible for health insurance benefits from Medicare or Medicaid.

Questions: Do you currently receive health insurance benefits?
If not, do you think you might be eligible for Medicare or Medicaid?

How can you advocate for yourself in the mental health system?

You may encounter a problem with the mental health system and may need to advocate for yourself. Here are some examples of problems that other people reported:

"I was on an endless list to see an individual counselor."

"I wanted to get a job. I couldn't find out how to get help with this."

"I was ready to leave the day treatment program, but people kept telling me there was no alternative."

When problems come up, the following guidelines may be helpful:

Keep a record of the details of the problem and what you have tried to do about it.

"I kept a copy of all my applications to the apartment program. Also, when I called someone at the housing office, I wrote down the date, who I spoke to, and what we talked about. I keep all the information together in a folder. It made it much easier to present my case to the apartment supervisor."

Seek out the person on your treatment team who has the most experience in the type of problem you are having.

"I was frustrated about finding a job. I found out from my case manager that there is an employment specialist on my treatment team. I asked my case manager to refer me to work with that person. It's moving the process along."

Talk about your concerns calmly and clearly.

"I was getting very impatient about getting into an apartment. At first I used to get furious when I saw the housing coordinator in the hall. She was very uncomfortable when I raised my voice. Then I tried asking for an appointment and speaking more calmly. I even rehearsed what I was going to say before I went in. She was much more responsive."

If you are not satisfied after speaking with the appropriate person, take additional action.

"Sometimes I don't get results from talking to the designated person. I have learned to ask to speak to their supervisor or to go to the consumer advocate. Getting them involved usually helps."

Follow through on actions that are your responsibility.

"When I went to the social worker about getting Social Security Disability (SSDI), he told me that I needed to get my employment records organized and bring them in so he could help me make the best case. I was the only one who knew where my records were, so if I didn't bring them in, my social worker couldn't proceed."

Let people know that you appreciate their efforts.

"The nurse was pleased when I told her that I had tried her suggestions for coping with some of the side effects of my medication. She asked me to let her know if there was anything else I needed."

If at first you don't succeed, try, try again.

"I had to be persistent about getting transportation to the Artists-in-Recovery program. At first people said it wasn't possible. But I was determined to attend the program, because I knew it was helping me. So I kept pursuing it, and I got other people to speak up for me. I finally got transportation."

Speak up for yourself if you encounter a problem in the mental health system.

Questions: Have you advocated for yourself in the mental health system?
If so, was it effective?

Who can you ask for help if you have a problem with the mental health system?

Mental health systems can seem huge and overwhelming. Even when you speak up for yourself, there may be times when it's helpful to have someone to help you advocate for yourself.

In many mental health systems, someone is designated as a "consumer advocate" or "complaint investigator" to help people with problems they might be having with the system. It is a good idea to get to know the consumer advocate at your Mental Health Center. In some states, there is a state office of consumer affairs or consumer advocacy. It is useful to learn how to access this resource also. Often these offices have a staff that includes people who have experienced psychiatric symptoms who are working as advocates. They can help answer your questions and guide you though the advocacy process.

Sometimes people feel that they "get lost in the system." To avoid that experience, it usually helps to find someone on your treatment team whom you feel comfortable talking to and whom you could turn to for help if you are having problems.

People usually feel most comfortable talking to someone who listens to their problems, asks questions, remembers what was said in past conversations, offers suggestions, and avoids critical or judgmental comments. Most people look for someone who seems to take an active interest in their well being.

The job title of the person with whom you feel comfortable will vary. Some people feel most comfortable talking with their case manager or their social worker or their psychiatrist. Other people feel most comfortable with their nurse or their psychologist or some other mental health worker.

Once you identify the person you feel comfortable with, it helps to keep him or her informed about how things are going with you. Let the person know both when things are going well and when things are not going well. Maintaining good communication will help the person be more effective if a problem comes up for you.

> *Get to know the consumer advocate at your mental health center.*

> *Identify someone on your treatment team to help you advocate for yourself if you encounter a problem with the mental health system.*

Questions: Do you know the consumer advocate at your community mental health center? Who on your treatment team would you like to help you advocate for yourself?

Are your needs being met by the mental health system?

You may or may not feel that your needs are being met by the mental health system. Answering the questions in the following chart could be helpful:

Questions About What I Receive From The Mental Health System

Questions	Answers (please be specific)
Are there additional services that I would like to receive? (see the "Mental Health Services Checklist," earlier in this handout)	
Are there any financial benefits that I would like to apply for?	
Are there any health insurance benefits I would like to apply for?	
Are there any food or nutrition programs that I would like to apply for?	
Are there any housing programs or benefits that I would like to apply for?	
Would I like to strengthen my skills at advocating for myself?	
Would I like to meet the consumer advocate at my mental health center or get to know him or her better?	
Would I like to identify someone on my treatment team who could help me advocate for myself?	
Is there anything else I would like to improve about what I receive from the mental health system?	

Summary of the main points about getting your needs met in the mental health system:

- Community mental health centers are the main source of public outpatient mental health services.

- Mental health centers usually offer a wide range of services.

- Individuals vary widely in the mental health services they use.

- Depending on your work history and financial need, you may be eligible for financial benefits from Social Security Disability Insurance (SSDI), Supplemental Security Income (SSI), or Public Assistance.

- Depending on your work history and financial need, you may be eligible for health insurance benefits from Medicare or Medicaid.

- Speak up for yourself if you encounter a problem in the mental health system.

- Get to know the consumer advocate at your mental health center.

- Identify someone on your treatment team to help you advocate for yourself if you encounter a problem with the mental health system.

NOTES

www.ingramcontent.com/pod-product-compliance
Lightning Source LLC
Chambersburg PA
CBHW081718100526
44591CB00016B/2412